THE TRIAL

FRANZ KAFKA

ADAPTED BY NICK GILL

Law Student / Flogger	**Marc Antolin**
Uncle Albert / Magistrate	**Steven Beard**
Male Guard / Assistant / Tudor	**Richard Cant**
Mrs Barrow / Information Officer	**Sarah Crowden**
Bank Clerk / Defendant in Tattooist	**Charlie Folorunsho**
Bank Clerk / Defendant in Information Office	**Neil Haigh**
Bank Clerk / Faye / Phone Voice	**Suzy King**
Josef K	**Rory Kinnear**
Tiffany / Female Guard / Rosa / Chastity / Cherry / Girl	**Kate O'Flynn**
Comptroller / Bank Clerk / Defendant	**Weruche Opia**
Kyle / Block	**Hugh Skinner**
Mrs Grace / Doctor	**Sian Thomas**

Direction	**Richard Jones**
Design	**Miriam Buether**
Costumes	**Nicky Gillibrand**
Light	**Mimi Jordan Sherin**
Music	**David Sawer**
Sound	**David Sawer & Alex Twiselton**
Movement	**Sarah Fahie**
Casting	**Julia Horan CDG**
Hair, Wigs & Make-Up Design	**Campbell Young Associates**
Fights	**Bret Yount**
Jerwood Assistant Director	**Nel Crouch**
Boris Karloff Trainee Assistant Director	**Robert Awosusi**

Young Vic community participants include: **Annie Greenslade, Antony Hampton, Barry Bowden, Boma Braide, Carol Morgan, Caroline Smith, Catherine Coker, Christina Christofi, David Mills, Declan Cooke, Drew Paterson, Jackie Kearns, Jan Teeuwisse, John Hellings, John S Watts, Kevin Bourke, Mable Muir, Michael Knight-Markiegi, Patricia Fryd, Peter Stanton, Robert Moore, Rod Brown, Stella Lee, Thelma Gordon, Val Harvey, Vince Rogers.**

Stage Manager	**Daniel Gammon**
Deputy Stage Manager	**Charlotte Hall**
Assistant Stage Managers	**Sally Inch**
	Greg Sharman
Costumer Supervisor	**Claire Murphy**
Props Supervisor	**Jo Maund**
Lighting Operator	**Sebastian Barresi /**
	Jess Glaisher
Sound Operator	**Amy Bramma /**
	Jamie McIntyre
Automation Operators	**Nell Allen**
	Zoë Cotton
Stage Crew	**Matt Fletcher**
Wardrobe Manager	**Heather Bull**
Wardrobe Assistant & Dresser	**Claire Wardroper**
Hair, Wigs & Make-Up	**Jenny Glynn**
Costume Assistant	**Rosey Morling**
Costume Makers	**Mark Costello**
	Phil Reynolds
Draughtsman	**Simon Oliver**
Stage Management Placement	**Deborah Machin**
Set built by	**Miraculous Engineering Ltd**
Automation supplied by	**Canning Conveyors**
	Stage Technologies
Lighting equipment supplied by	**Stage Electrics**
Sound equipment supplied by	**Stage Sound Services**

Nel Crouch is supported through the Jerwood Assistant Directors Program at the Young Vic.

Robert Awosusi is supported through the Boris Karloff Trainee Assistant Directors Program at the Young Vic.

With generous support from The Richenthal Foundation.

We would like to thank James Hawes, Gareth Damian Martin, National Theatre Video Department, Gail at Essentially Eagle Vintage, Russell Beck, Vicky Fifield, Douglas Henn-Macrae at DHMidi Organs, Scott Farrell at Rochester Cathedral and Copperfield Rehearsal Rooms SE1.

Biographies

FRANZ KAFKA

Kafka was born into a middle-class Jewish family in Prague in 1883. In 1906 he received a Law degree from Prague's Deutsche Universität. By this time he had written many stories, sketches, prose poems and fragments of novels. He wrote prolifically, supporting himself by means of a job in insurance.

By the time of his death from tuberculosis in 1924, he had published little and his work was known to few. He left his manuscripts to his friend Max Brod with instructions to burn them unread. Brod however arranged for the publication of his work, including *The Trial* which he compiled from the fragments Kafka had left unfinished.

Taken together, his major works – *The Trial* and *The Castle* as well as his many stories and fragments, his diaries and letters and his famous "Letter to His Father" – all make him unquestionably one of the most acclaimed and influential writers of the 20th century.

NICK GILL

Nick is a playwright, musician and composer.

Theatre includes: *beneverunerstoost* (Royal Court); *Sand* (Royal Court); *fiji land* (Southwark Playhouse); *Mirror Teeth* (Finborough); and various shorts written as part of The Apathists, 2006-7.

Music for theatre, film, radio and live performance includes: *Thrown* (Royal Court); *In Eldersfield: Chapter 2* (Kings of England); *One Million* (Tangled Feet); *Knock Out* (Deutschlandradio Kultur) and *Blasted* (The Other Room).

He is currently working on a new album by his seven piece instrumental group, The Monroe Transfer.

RICHARD JONES – Direction

Previous Young Vic includes: *Public Enemy, The Government Inspector, Annie Get Your Gun, The Good Soul of Szechuan, Hobson's Choice* and *Six Characters Looking For An Author.*

Other theatre includes: work directed at The Old Vic, The National Theatre, RSC, Ambassadors / Royal Court and in the West End.

In New York, theatre includes the Public Theater and three titles on Broadway.

Opera includes: work at the Royal Opera House, ENO, Glyndebourne, WNO, The Met, La Scala as well as in Paris, Berlin, Chicago, Munich, Frankfurt and Aix en Provence.

Awards include: Olivier Awards for *Too Clever By Half* (Old Vic); *Into the Woods* (West End); *The Trojans* and *The Mastersingers of Nuremberg* (ENO); *Lady Macbeth of Mtsensk* (Royal Opera House) and *Hansel and Gretel* (WNO). Evening Standard Awards for *The Illusion* (Old Vic) and *The Ring* (Royal Opera House); Tony nomination for *La Bete* (Eugene O'Neill Theater, New York).

Richard was appointed Commander of the Order of the British Empire (CBE) in the 2015 New Year's Honours.

MIRIAM BUETHER – Design

Previous Young Vic includes: *Public Enemy, Wild Swans* (2013 Critics' Circle Award), *The Government Inspector, In the Red and Brown Water, The Good Soul Of Szechuan* and *Generations*.

Theatre includes: *Sunny Afternoon, Chariots of Fire* (Hampstead, West End); *The Father* (Theatre Royal Bath and Tricycle Theatre); *Decade* (Headlong); *Earthquakes in London* (2010 Evening Standard Award), *The Effect* (National Theatre); *Sucker Punch* (2010 Evening Standard Award), *In The Republic of Happiness, Love and Information, Cock, Get Santa!* (Royal Court); *Game, Judgement Day* (Almeida); *Six Characters in Search of an Author* (Chichester, West End) and *Guantanamo: Honor Bound to Defend Freedom* (Tricycle, West End, New York and San Francisco).

Opera includes: *The Girl of the Golden West* (ENO); *Anna Nicole (also in New York)* and *Il Trittico / Suor Angelica* (Royal Opera House).

Additional awards include: 2008 Hospital Club Creative Award for Theatre; overall winner of The Linbury Prize for Stage Design in 1999.

NICKY GILLIBRAND – Costumes

Previous Young Vic includes: *Public Enemy, Hamlet, The Government Inspector, Annie Get Your Gun, The Good Soul of Szechuan, Vernon God Little* and *King Lear*.

Other theatre includes: *Everyman, The Seagull, Tales from the Vienna Wood* (National Theatre); *In Basildon* (Royal Court); *Billy Elliot* (West End, Broadway, Chicago, Australia); *Wind in the Willows* (Duchess Theatre in 2013 – Olivier nomination Best Costume Design, also at Vaudeville Theatre in 2014); *The Tempest* and *A Midsummer Night's Dream* (RSC).

Opera includes: *Anna Nicole* (also in New York), *Il Trittico, L'Heure Espagnole/Gianni Schicchi, Lady Macbeth of Mtsensk* (Royal Opera House); *The Girl of the Golden West, Rodelinda, The Magic Flute, Cavalleria rusticana / Pagliacci, Don Giovanni, Peter Grimes* (ENO); *Die Zauberflote* (ENO, Amsterdam, Aix Festival); *Midsummer Marriage* (Munich); *Der Rosenkavalier, Miserly Knight, Gianni Schicchi* (Glyndebourne) and *War and Peace* (Paris).

Awards include: The Gold award for Best Costume Design, Prague Quadrenale 2003 for *A Midsummer Night's Dream* for the Royal Shakespeare Company.

MIMI JORDAN SHERIN – Light

Previous Young Vic includes: *Annie Get Your Gun, The Government Inspector, Enemy of the People* and *Lost Highway*.

Other theatre includes: Productions at The Royal Court, The Old Vic, The National, The RSC and in the West End.

Opera includes: *Anna Nicole Smith, Gloriana, The Gambler, Gianni Schicchi / L'Heure Espagnole, Lady Macbeth of Mtsensk* (Royal Opera House); *Meistersinger, Rodelinda, Fanciulla Del West, Paglliacci / Cavalleria, Petra Von Kant, Morning to Midnight* (ENO); *Der Rosenkavalier, Falstaff, Flight* (Glyndebourne); *Peter Grimes* (La Scala); *Lohengrin, Tales of Hoffman, Guilio Cesare* (Munich); *Jenufa* (Vienna); *Makropulos Case, Billy Budd* (Frankfurt); *Katya Kabanova* (La Fenice) and *Lulu* (New Tokyo Opera).

Mimi's American theatre work includes designs for Broadway and multiple regional theatres.

For her work in New York she has been awarded the American Theatre Wing award, two Obies, an Eddy award, a Tony nomination and five Drama Desk nominations.

DAVID SAWER – Music & Sound

Previous Young Vic includes: *The Good Soul of Szechuan, Government Inspector* and *Public Enemy.*

Other works include: *Caravanserai, The Lighthouse Keepers, Rumpelstiltskin, The Memory of Water* (BCMG); *Coachman Chronos* (NMC/Aurora Orchestra); *Bronze and Iron* (Onyx Brass / NMBiennale); *Flesh and Blood, Trumpet Concerto* (BBC Symphony Orchestera); *Skin Deep* (Opera North/Bregenz Festival/Royal Danish Opera, Copenhagen); *Piano Concerto* (British Composer Award 2002), *Byrnan Wood* (BBC Proms); *Rebus* (musikFabrik); *From Morning to Midnight* (ENO); *Tiroirs* (London Sinfonietta); *the greatest happiness principle* (BBC National Orchestra of Wales); *Songs of Love and War* (BBC Singers); *Hollywood Extra* (Matrix Ensemble) and *Cat's-eye* (Lontano/Ballet Rambert).

Other theatre includes: *Hamlet* (RSC); *The Blue Ball* (National Theatre); *Food of Love* (Almeida) and *Jackets* (Bush).

Radio includes: *Swansong* (Sony Radio Award) and *The Long Time Ago Story* (BBC Radio 3).

ALEX TWISELTON – Sound

Previous Young Vic includes: *A View from the Bridge* (also Wyndham's), *Oh My Sweet Land, Safe House* and *Sizwe Banzi Is Dead.*

Other theatre includes: *Little Shop of Horrors, A Man of No Importance, Dangerous Corner, Anne* and *Zef, Stepping Out, Epsom Downs, Blackbird, Death and the Maiden, A Taste of Honey, A Game of Love and Chance, The Country and Faith Healer* (Salisbury Playhouse); *Toro! Toro!* (Poonamallee Productions) and *The Girl in the Yellow Dress* (Theatre503).

Theatre as an Associate Sound Designer includes: *Our Country's Good* (Out of Joint, UK and USA tour).

SARAH FAHIE – Movement

Opera includes: *The Gambler, Il Tabarro, Suor Angelica* (Royal Opera House); *Peter Grimes* (La Scala); *Rodelinda* (ENO); *Der Rosenkavalier* (Glyndebourne); *Aida* (Royal Albert Hall); *Capriccio* (Grange Park Opera); *The Bartered Bride* (Mid Wales Opera); *La Traviata, La Boheme* (Opera Holland Park); *As I Crossed a Bridge of Dreams* (Almeida); *The Birds* (The Opera Group); *Hansel and Gretel* (Garsington Opera) and *Don Giovanni* (Bergen Opera).

Sarah has also worked as an Associate / Revival director on *Rumpelstiltskin* (BCMG) and *Falstaff* (Glyndebourne).

JULIA HORAN CDG – Casting

Julia is an Associate Artist at the Young Vic.

Previous Young Vic includes: *Ah, Wilderness!, Happy Days, Man: Three plays by Tennessee Williams, A View from the Bridge* (also Wyndham's), *Public Enemy, The Shawl, Blackta, A Doll's House* (also Duke of York's/BAM), *After Miss Julie, Government Inspector, The Events* (also ATC), *Wild Swans* (also ART) *Joe Turner's Come and Gone, Glass Menagerie* and *Annie Get Your Gun.*

Other theatre includes: *Medea, Oresteia, Game, Mr Burns, Chimerica, Before the Party, King Lear, Children's Children, The Homecoming* (Almeida); *Hope, Teh Internet* is *Serious Business*, *Wolf from the Door*, *The Nether* (also Duke of York's), *Adler & Gibb*, *Birdland*, *Khandan*, *The Mistress Contract*, *The Pass*, *Wastwater*, *Tribes*, *Clybourne Park* (also Wyndham's), *Spur of the Moment*, *Sucker Punch* (Royal Court); *Hamlet* (Barbican); S*pring Awakening*, *The Seagull* (Headlong); *The Lighthouse Keeper* (BCMG); *Red Velvet* (Tricycle / St Ann's Warehouse); *A Chorus of Disapproval*, *Absent Friends* (Harold Pinter); *Backbeat* (Duke of York's, Toronto & LA) and *Krapp's Last Tape / A Kind of Alaska* (Bristol Old Vic).

CAMPBELL YOUNG ASSOCIATES – Hair, Wigs & Make-Up Design

Previous Young Vic includes: *Public Enemy, A Doll's House, Three Sisters, Wild Swans, Hamlet, Government Inspector, Annie Get Your Gun, The Good Soul of Szechuan, Vernon God Little* and *Six Characters Looking for an Author.*

Other theatre includes: *Bend It Like Beckham, Taken At Midnight, Made in Dagenham, Gypsy, Henry V, Stephen Ward, Passion Play, Peter and Alice, Old Times, Charlie and the Chocolate Factory, The Bodyguard, Hay Fever, The King's Speech, Sweeney Todd, Betrayal, The Children's Hour, Love Never Dies, Breakfast at Tiffany's, Priscilla, Oliver!* (West End); *High Society, Clarence Darrow, Sweet Bird of Youth, Richard III, Inherit the Wind* (Old Vic); *City of Angels* (Donmar); *The Cripple of Inishmaan, Matilda, Ghost, Private Lives, La Bête, Billy Elliot* (West End/Broadway); *A Delicate Balance, It's Only A Play, The Last Ship, Betrayal, Les Misérables, One Man, Two Guvnors* and *Spider-Man* (Broadway).

NEL CROUCH – Assistant Director

Theatre Includes: *Launch Party* (R&D, Farnham Maltings); *Lorraine & Alan* (Edinburgh Fringe / Battersea Arts Centre / National Tour); *The Beasts* (Lyric Hammersmith, GDIF, Imagine Watford, Latitude); *The Long Trick* (R&D, Nightingale Theatre); *Drone* (Theatre503); *Speak, Memory* (Ovalhouse); *Festen* (Wickham Theatre) and *Yellow Moon* (Alma Tavern / Edinburgh Fringe).

Theatre as an assistant includes: *What the Thunder Said* (Theatre Centre); *Home* (Arcola) and *Found at Sea* (Traverse).

Nel is artistic director of Bucket Club, an associate company of Farnham Maltings. They are the first recipients of the Farnham Maltings Fellowship. Nel is a 2015 BBC Performing Arts Fund Fellow and will become Director in Residence at the Tobacco Factory Theatres under the scheme in August.

She has worked as a Young Company assistant at the Unicorn Theatre. She is a graduate of the Royal Court's Introduction to Playwriting Group.

JERWOOD **CHARITABLE** FOUNDATION

ROBERT AWOSUSI – Trainee Assistant Director

Theatre includes: *Housekeeping* (Animals: Rapid Write Response at Theatre503); *Dumb Muscle* (Playground at The Horse and Stables); and *The Country* (University of Hull).

Robert is also a playwright and poet.

Robert is supported through the Boris Karloff Trainee Assistant Director Program at the Young Vic.

CAST

MARC ANTOLIN – Law Student / Flogger

Theatre includes: *Taken at Midnight* (Chichester Minerva, Theatre Royal Haymarket); *Amadeus, Singin' In The Rain, The Music Man* (Chichester Festival); *From Here to Eternity* (Shaftesbury); *Matilda* (RSC/Cambridge Theatre); *Bells Are Ringing, Once Upon a Time at the Adelphi* (Union); *Into The Woods, Hello Dolly,* (Regent's Park Open Air Theatre); *Billy Liar* (UK tour) and *Imagine This* (New London Theatre).

Film includes: *London Road, Coconut Shy, Hunky Dory* and *Love Actually.*

Television includes: *Caerdydd* and *More Than Love.*

STEVEN BEARD – Uncle Albert / Magistrate

Previous Young Vic includes: *The Good Soul of Szechuan* and *The Government Inspector.*

Theatre includes: *The Crucible* (West Yorkshire Playhouse); *A Flea in her Ear, The Illusion* (Old Vic); *Uncle Vanya, The Winter's Tale, The Bald Prima Donna, The Breasts of Tiresias, The Park* (Crucible, Sheffield); *The Lady From the Sea, The Father* (Citizens Theatre, Glasgow); *Waiting for Godot* (Belgrade Theatre, Coventry); *Endgame* (Nottingham Playhouse, Weimar 1999); *Nathan the Wise, The Seagull, Seven Doors, Scapino* (Chichester Festival); *Racing Demon, Le Bourgeois Gentilhomme, A Midsummer Night's Dream* (National Theatre); *Of Thee I Sing, Let 'em Eat Cake* and *Paradise Moscow* (Opera North).

Film includes: *Anna Karenina, The Remains of the Day* and *Shakespeare in Love.*

RICHARD CANT – Male Guard / Assistant / Tudor

Theatre includes: *My Night with Reg* (Donmar/Apollo); *War Horse* (National Theatre); *Salome* (Headlong); *Troilus and Cressida, Cymbeline, As You Like It* (Cheek By Jowl); *The Country Wife, Original Sin* (Sheffield Crucible); *She Stoops to Conquer* (New Kent Opera); *Pera Pelas* (Gate); *Other People* (Royal Court); *Angels in America* (Manchester Library); *Hamlet, Cymbeline, Much Ado About Nothing* (RSC); *The Modern Husband* (Actors Touring Co.); *The Canterbury Tales* (Garrick) and *Waterland* (Eastern Angles).

Film includes: *Sparkle* and *Lawless Heart.*

Television includes: *Mapp And Lucia, Outlander, Above Suspicion: Red Dahlia, Doctor Who, Vexed, The Bill, Midsomer Murders, Bleak House, Gunpowder, Treason & Plot, The Way We Live Now, Shackleton, Gimme Gimme Gimme, Sunburn, This Life* and *Great Expectations.*

Radio and Voice includes: *Medieval Hitchhiker, Assassin's Creed, 007 Legends.*

SARAH CROWDEN – Mrs Barrow / Information Officer

Theatre includes: *Flare Path* (Theatre Royal, Haymarket); *If So, Then Yes* (Jermyn Street); *Little Women* (Duchess); *20,000 Leagues Under The Sea* (Stratford East); *The Man Who Came To Dinner* (Chichester Festival); *The Flag* (Moving Theatre); *Chatsky* (Almeida & tour); *La Bete* (Lyric Hammersmith); *Rookery Nook* (Greenwich) and *A Midsummer Night's Dream* (RSC, Stratford, tour and London).

Film includes: *Alice Through the Looking Glass, Queen of the Desert, The Riot Club, Jupiter Ascending, Quartet, Brideshead Revisited, The Oxford Murders, Miss Potter, The*

Man Who Knew Too Little, Orlando, Erik the Viking and *The Wind in the Willows.*

Television includes: *Doc Martin, New Tricks, Cockroaches, Wolf Hall, Downton Abbey, Doctors, Endeavour, Upstairs Downstairs, Affinity, The Sarah Jane Adventures, Longford, He Knew He Was Right, Tipping the Velvet* and *Vanity Fair.*

Sarah is also a book reviewer and writer. She has reviewed for The Lady, TLS and Literary Review amongst others, and contributes regularly to the literary quarterly Slightly Foxed.

CHARLIE FOLORUNSHO – Bank Clerk / Defendant in Tattooist

Previous Young Vic includes: *The Mosquito Coast.*

Other theatre includes: *Satyagraha* (ENO & Metropolitan Opera, New York); *The Firework Maker's Daughter* (Lyric Hammersmith); *Gilgamesh* (London Parks); *All's Well That Ends Well* (UK tour); *The Lower Depths* (The Clink Vaults); *Muhummad Ali & Me* (Ovalhouse); *Under Their Influence* (Tricycle); *The Southwark Mysteries* (Southwark Cathedral), *Faust* (UK tour); *The Tempest* (Brighton Beach); *And the Snake Shed its Skin* (Oxford Playhouse); *Slamdunk* (Hackney Empire); *The Resistible Rise of Artuto Ui* (Mercury); *Peter Pan* (Sheffield Crucible); *A Mad World My Masters* (New Wolsey); *The Arrival* (Newcastle Playhouse); *Momo* (Greenwich Theatre); *Romeo & Juliet* (Duke's Playhouse); *The Evocation of Papa Mas* (Theatre Royal, Plymouth); *Fermentation* (Edinburgh, The Underbelly); *Brave New World* (European Tour) and *The Jungle Book* (Theatre Royal, Basingstoke).

NEIL HAIGH – Bank Clerk / Defendant in Information Office

Theatre includes: *World Cup 66* (Bristol Old Vic); *What The Dickens* (Brewery, Bristol), *Pub Rock, Hard Hearted Hannah* (also Kennedy Center Washington DC) (Lyric Hammersmith); *Made Up* (Soho Theatre); *The Summer House, Difficulty of Concentration, Angels of the Universe* (Gate); *Mass Observation* (Edinburgh International Festival); *The Irish Giant* (Southwalk Playhouse); *The Ratcatcher of Hamelin, Meat & Two Veg* (BAC); *A Midsummer Night's Dream* (UK Tour) and *Ether Frolics* (SHUNT / Sound & Fury).

Television includes: *Dalziel and Pascoe, No Angels, Casualty, The Bill* and *Doctors* (National Soap Award nomination 2014).

SUZY KING – Bank Clerk / Faye / Phone Voice

Theatre includes: *Swanwhite* (Gate); *Merry Christmas Mr Burbage* (Theatre, Shoreditch); *Dr Faustus, Daisy Pulls It Off* (Dukes, Lancaster); *The Millionairess* (BAC); *Marya, A Flea in Her Ear* (Old Vic) and *Gala / Dali* (Old Red Lion).

Opera credits include: *Anna Nicole, Il Trittico, The Gambler, Lady Macbeth of Mtsensk* (Royal Opera House); *Der Rosenkavalier, Falstaff* (Glyndebourne); *Julietta, Lulu, Die Fledermaus* and *Don Carlos* (ENO).

Film includes: *The Third Party, Like It Is* and *Knickers.*

Television includes: *Chandler & Co., Anna Lee, The Upper Hand, The House of Eliot, Blood Rights, Sixth Sense, Style Monsters, Star Wars* and *The Esther Show.*

Suzy's radio credits include work as a presenter for Zimbabwe Broadcasting Corporation Radio 1.

RORY KINNEAR – Josef K

Theatre includes: *Othello, The Last of the Haussmans, Hamlet, Burnt By The Sun, The Revenger's Tragedy, Philistines, The Man of Mode, Southwark Fair* (National Theatre); *Measure For Measure* (Almeida); *Mary Stuart* (Donmar); *Festen* (Lyric Hammersmith); *Hamlet* (Old Vic); *Cymbeline, The Taming of the Shrew* (RSC); *The Tempest* (Theatre Royal Plymouth) and *The Seagull* (Theatre Royal Northampton).

Film includes: *The Imitation Game, Cuban Fury, Skyfall, Broken, Wild Target* and *Quantum of Solace*.

Television includes: *The Casual Vacancy, Penny Dreadful, Lucan, Count Arthur Strong, Southcliffe, Loving Miss Hatto, Richard II, Black Mirror: National Anthem, Edwin Drood, Lennon Naked, First Men, Vexed, Cranford, Beautiful People, The Thick Of It, Waking the Dead, Ashes To Ashes, Minder, Stepoe and Sons, Plus One, Messiah V, The Long Walk to Finchley, Mansfield Park, Five Days, Secret Smile, Silent Witness, Second Coming* and *Menace*.

KATE O'FLYNN – Tiffany / Female Guard / Rosa / Chastity / Cherry / Girl

Theatre includes: *A Taste of Honey, Port* (National Theatre); *The Ritual Slaughter of Gorge Mastromas, A Miracle* (Royal Court); *Lungs, The Sound of Heavy Rain* (Paines Plough / Sheffield); *Marine Parade* (ETT); *The Whisky Taster* (Bush); *House of Special Purpose* (Chichester Minerva); *See How they Run* and *The Children's Hour* (Manchester Royal Exchange).

Film includes: *Mr Turner, Up There* and *Happy Go Lucky*.

Television includes: *Not You Again, Ordinary Lies, No Offence, New Tricks, Room at the Top, Playhouse Presents: The Snipist, Above Suspicion, The Syndicate, The Suspicions of Mr Whicher, Kingdom, The Palace* and *Trial and Retribution*.

WERUCHE OPIA – Comptroller / Bank Clerk / Defendant

Theatre includes: *Liberian Girl* (Royal Court); *The Waiting Room, For Coloured Girls, The Inheritors* (National Theatre, Nigeria) and *Shakespeare Sonnets* (The Globe).

Film includes: *Bad Education The Movie* and *When Love Happens*.

Television includes: *Bad Education: Series Three, Banana, Suspects, Gum, Top Boy: Series 2, Million Pound Squat* and *The Bill*.

HUGH SKINNER – Kyle / Block

Previous Young Vic includes: *The Cherry Orchard* and *Señora Carrar's Rifles*.

Other theatre includes: *Thérèse Raquin* (Theatre Royal Bath); *American Psycho* (Almeida); *Pastoral* (Soho); *Wild Oats* (Bristol Old Vic); *You Can't Take It With You* (Manchester Royal Exchange); *66 Books, Where's My Seat?, 2 May 1997, SuddenLossOfDignity.com* (Bush); *'Tis Pity She's A Whore* (Liverpool Everyman); *Is Everyone OK?* (Nabokov); *The Great Game* (Tricycle); *Angry Young Man* (Trafalgar Studios); *The Enchantment* (National Theatre) and *French Without Tears* (English Touring Theatre).

Film includes: *Kill Your Friends, Les Miserables* and *Day of the Dead*.

Television includes: *W1A, Fleabag, Bugsplat, Our Zoo, Wipers Times, Law & Order, Any Human Heart, Tess of the D'Urbervilles* and *Bonkers*.

SIAN THOMAS – Mrs Grace / Doctor

Previous Young Vic includes: *Rainsnakes.*

Other theatre includes: *Minetti* (Barbican / Royal Lyceum Edinburgh); *Eldorado, Small Craft Warnings* (Arcola); *Passion Play* (Duke of York's); *Blue Heart Afternoon, Feelgood* (also Garrick), *The Glass Room* (Hampstead); *Richard II* (Donmar); *Brittanicus* (Wilton's Music Hall); *Who's Afraid of Virginia Woolf* (Northern Stage / Sheffield Crucible); *The Goat* (Traverse); *Spring Awakening* (Lyric Hammersmith and Novello); *Fram, House and Garden, Sleep With Me, Richard II, The Way of the World* (National Theatre); *Ghosts* (Bristol Old Vic); *Macbeth, Hamlet* (RSC / Albery Theatre); *The Price* (Apollo / Tricycle); *Push Up, Bloody Poetry* (Royal Court); *King Lear, Richard III* (also Savoy), *Happy End* and *Taming of the Shrew* (RSC) and *Up for Grabs* (Wyndham's – Olivier Award nominated).

Film includes: *Harry Potter and the Half-Blood Prince, Harry Potter and the Order of the Phoenix, Perfume, Vanity Fair, Rose Red, Erik the Viking* and *Prick Up Your Ears.*

Television includes: *Atlantis, New Tricks, Merlin, The Royal Bodyguard, Syrinx, Thinspiration, Half Broken Things* and *Lewis.*

Young Vic
It's a big world in here

Our shows
We present the widest variety of classics, new plays, forgotten works and music theatre. We tour and co-produce extensively within the UK and internationally.

Our artists
Our shows are created by some of the world's great theatre people alongside the most adventurous of the younger generation. This fusion makes the Young Vic one of the most exciting theatres in the world.

Our audience
...is famously the youngest and most diverse in London. We encourage those who don't think theatre is 'for them' to make it part of their lives. We give 10% of our tickets to schools and neighbours irrespective of box office demand, and keep prices low.

Our partners near at hand
Each year we engage with 10,000 local people – individuals and groups of all kinds including schools and colleges – by exploring theatre on and off stage. From time to time we invite our neighbours to appear on our stage alongside professionals.

Our partners further away
By co-producing with leading theatre, opera, and dance companies from London and around the world we create shows neither partner could achieve alone.

The Cut Bar & Restaurant
Our bar and restaurant is a relaxing place to meet and eat. An inspired mix of classic and original play-themed dishes made from fresh, free-range and organic ingredients creates an exciting menu. **www.thecutbar.com**

The Young Vic is a company limited by guarantee, registered in England No. 1188209.

VAT registration No. 236 673 348

The Young Vic (registered charity number 268876) receives public funding from:

Get more from the Young Vic Online

 youngvictheatre

 @youngvictheatre

 youngviclondon

 youngviclondon.wordpress.com

 @youngvictheatre

Sign up to receive email updates at **youngvic.org/register**

Get involved with the Young Vic

To produce our sell-out, award-winning shows and provide thousands of free activities through our Taking Part programme requires major investment. Find out how you can make a difference and get involved.

As an individual... become a Friend to jump the queues, a Soul Mate to go behind the scenes, donate to a special project, or remember the Young Vic in your will.

As a company... take advantage of our flexible memberships, exciting sponsorship opportunities, corporate workshops and CSR engagement.

As a trust or foundation... support our innovative and forward-thinking programmes on stage and off.

Are you interested in events... hire a space in our award-winning building and we can work with you to create truly memorable workshops, conferences or parties.

For more information visit

youngvic.org/support us

020 7922 2810

Registered charity (no. 268876)

Supporting the Young Vic

The Young Vic relies on the generous support of many individuals, trusts, foundations, and companies to produce our work, on and off stage. For their recent support we thank

Public Funders
Arts Council England
British Council
Creative & Cultural Skills
Lambeth Borough Council
Southwark Council

Corporate Partners
Barclays
Berkeley Group
Bloomberg
Edelman
Markit
Taylor Wessing LLP
Wahaca

Corporate Members
aka
Bloomberg
Clifford Chance
Edelman
Ingenious Media PLC
Mishcon de Reya
Royal Bank Of Scotland
and NatWest
Wisdom Council

**Partners &
Upper Circle**
David and Corinne Abbott
Tony & Gisela Bloom
Patrick Handley
Jack & Linda Keenan
Chris & Jane Lucas
Patrick McKenna
Simon & Midge Palley
Karl-Johan Persson
Jon & NoraLee Sedmak
Dasha Shenkman
Rita & Paul Skinner
Bruno Wang
Anda & Bill Winters

Soul Mates
Ensemble
Guy America & Dominique Bellec
Royce & Rotha Bell
Beatrice Bondy
Caroline & Ian Cormack
Jill and Jack Gerber
Manfred and Lydia Gorvy
Jill & Justin Manson
Miles Morland
Rob & Lesley O'Rahilly
Olga Slater
Catherine Schreiber
Justin Shinebourne
Sir Patrick Stewart
Edgar & Judith Wallner

Jane Attias
Liza Bartfield & Bill Updegraff
Chris & Frances Bates
Anthony & Karen Beare
Joanne Beckett
The Bickertons
Sarah Billinghurst Solomon
Katie Bradford
CJ & LM Braithwaite
Sandra Carlisle
Tim & Caroline Clark
Kay Ellen Consolver
Felicia Crystal
Miel de Botton
Lucy & Spencer de Grey
Robyn Durie
Sean Egan
Jennifer & Jeff Eldredge
Don Ellwood &
Sandra Johnigan
Gillian Frumkin
Paul Gambaccini
Beth & Gary Glynn
Sarah Gay Fletcher
Rory Godson
Annika Goodwille
Sarah Hall
Caroline Hansberry
Richard Hardman & Family
Madeleine Hodgkin
Nik Holttum & Helen Brannigan
Jane Horrocks
Miss Lottie Hughes
Maxine Isaacs
Clive Jones
Tom Keatinge
John Kinder & Gerry Downey
Carol Lake
Jude Law
Tony Mackintosh
James & Sue Macmillan
Karen McHugh
Ian McKellen
Barbara Minto
Ann & Gavin Neath CBE
Georgia Oetker
Powerscourt
Lady Rayne Lacey
Barbara Reeves
Anthony & Sally Salz
Nicola Stanhope
Jan & Michael Topham
Totally Theatre Productions
The Ulrich Family
The Ury Trust
Donna & Richard Vinter
Jimmy & Carol Walker
Rob Wallace

Trust Supporters
95.8 Capital FM's
Help a Capital Child
Amberstone Trust
Andor Charitable Trust
Austin & Hope Pilkington Trust
BBC Children in Need
Backstage Trust
Boris Karloff Foundation
Boshier Hinton Foundation
The City Bridge Trust
The Cleopatra Trust
Clifford Chance Foundation
Clore Duffield Foundation
John S Cohen Foundation
The Cooperative Membership
Community Fund
The Creative Employment
Programme
David Laing Foundation
The Dr. Mortimer and
Theresa Sackler Foundation
D'Oyly Carte Charitable Trust
Embassy of the Kingdom
of the Netherlands
Equitable Charitable Trust
The Eranda Foundation
Ernest Cook Trust
The Foyle Foundation
Garfield Weston Foundation
Garrick Charitable Trust
Genesis Foundation
Golden Bottle Trust
Golsoncott Foundation
The Harold Hyam Wingate Foundation
Jerwood Charitable Foundation
Joanies Fund
John Ellerman Foundation
John Thaw Foundation
J. Paul Getty Jnr
Charitable Trust
The Kidron and Hall Family
The Limbourne Trust
The Mackintosh Foundation
Martin Bowley Charitable Trust
Mrs Margaret Guido's
Charitable Trust
Newcomen Collett Foundation
The Noel Coward Foundation
The Nomura Charitable Trust
The Portrack Charitable Trust
The Rayne Trust
The Red Hill Trust
Richard Radcliffe
Charitable Trust
The Richenthal Foundation
Royal Norwegian Embassy
The Sackler Trust
Sir Walter St John's
Educational Charity
The Wolfson Foundation

*and all others who wish
to remain anonymous.*

markit

Proud to be the lead sponsor of the

Young Vic's Funded Ticket Programme

Enabling theatre to be enjoyed by all

markit.com

THE TRIAL

Franz Kafka

THE TRIAL

Adapted by Nick Gill

OBERON BOOKS
LONDON

WWW.OBERONBOOKS.COM

First published in 2015 by Oberon Books Ltd
521 Caledonian Road, London N7 9RH
Tel: +44 (0) 20 7607 3637 / Fax: +44 (0) 20 7607 3629
e-mail: info@oberonbooks.com
www.oberonbooks.com

A catalogue record for this book is available from the British
Library.

PB ISBN: 978-1-78319-878-8
E ISBN: 978-1-78319-879-5

Cover: Image by David Sandison
          Design by AKA

Typeset in Joanna by James Illman

Printed, bound and converted
by CPI Group (UK) Ltd, Croydon, CR0 4YY.

My thanks to David Lan, Richard Jones, Nick Quinn,
all at the Young Vic and, as ever, all The Apathists.

*For Ve, who was more help than she knows
and for Aphra, who was no help at all.*

nx

Characters

JOSEF K	GRACE
TIFFANY	FAYE
MRS BARROW	CHERRY
ROSA	MAGISTRATE
MALE GUARD	FLOGGER
FEMALE GUARD	STUDENT
COMPTROLLER	CHASTITY
RABENSTEIN	INFORMATION OFFICER
KAMINER	ASSISTANT
KULLYCH	GIRL
KYLE	TUDOR
VOICE	DOCTOR
ALBERT	

Various neighbours, bank employees, lawyers, Court members, defendants, club patrons and bystanders.

Rosa, Tiffany, Female guard, Cherry, Chastity & Girl should be played by the same actor.

Rabenstein, Kaminer & Kullych should at least appear to be played by the same actors throughout; after their first appearance, they are always present.

Notes on text

A line ending with an ellipsis […] indicates trailing off

A line ending with a dash [–] indicates interruption.

A forward slash [/] indicates the start of the next line of dialogue.

K's subvocal lines in italics are inaudible to anyone else.

At points, the script typographically gives the impression of a voice becoming less intelligible, without trying to prescribe its exact timing or how the effect should be achieved.

There were no stage directions in the rehearsal script; they are present in the playtext for ease of reading and to reflect Richard Jones's production.

TIFFANY dances for K; he pays her, and she leaves.

K wakes up in bed.

K

an almost woke ee up one morn – like baby
innocent an bold, the great white hole, lord of all
surveys, unslandered, clear of mind an hurt, future
ahead an ee all indestructible – Josef K

like crushed out dog on motorroad side

eyes a-glass an full of blood an vim for the day

im watched from all round windows, sunk all
stary eyes in bobby heads on spring, slobberjaw
an blanken lips

hello neighbours, distant dogs

not a wave

listen birds

observen through window neighbours

listen world go businessing in street

thinken wasted one more Tiffany night

thinken breakfast

thinken if ee can face to confront it all

an finally, procrast no more

bold im brass, shoulderwheel an steeled to task,
ee – Josef K – almost awake an greet

K   Rosa?

COMPTROLLER enters.

COMPTROLLER   Who's Rosa?

               Are you expecting Rosa?

K   No.

COMPTROLLER   You did just say 'Rosa', didn't you?

K   That's her flat. Who are you? What are you doing in there?

COMPTROLLER   She's not in. Is she always back this late?

K   She works at night. Are you with the police?

COMPTROLLER   She works at night?

9

K   Not like that.

COMPTROLLER   That's what you said.

K   She's a bartender, she comes home for breakfast; she should be back any minute, I'm sure she can answer all your questions then.

COMPTROLLER   You think we're here to talk to her?

K   Well, you're not here for me, are you?

Hang on ...

an while ee stand there all imperium, look for identity in all drawers, proof of adult an official, show im ee all aboveboard.

Here you go —

COMPTROLLER   What are those?

K   They were just in the drawer.

COMPTROLLER   You're saying someone filled your drawer with sweets?

K   I'm not saying anything; I'm just showing you my ID. If that's all, I'm going to have a shower.

COMPTROLLER   You said that was Rosa's room. Do you share a shower?

K   I wasn't going in, I just went near the door. You can't object to my taking a shower.

COMPTROLLER   Do you do anything objectionable?

K   I do the same as everyone else.

COMPTROLLER   And what does everyone else do?

K   I'm going to get dressed now.

COMPTROLLER   All right.

K   You want me to get undressed right here?

MALE GUARD enters.

MALE GUARD   Why are you getting undressed?

COMPTROLLER   Stay here.

COMPTROLLER leaves.

K   I'm not —

MALE GUARD	It won't help, he's not like that.
K	I was just pointing out that if he didn't leave, I couldn't get dressed.
MALE GUARD	He's gone now.
K	Yes, but you're here.
MALE GUARD	I don't follow.
K	I'm not getting dressed in front of you.
MALE GUARD	You said the Comptroller was the problem.
K	I would like it noted that I'm doing this under protest.
MALE GUARD	Sure.

K dresses and tries to leave. FEMALE GUARD enters.

FEMALE GUARD	Didn't he tell you to stay in your room?
MALE GUARD	He did, I heard him.
K	You are the police, aren't you?
FEMALE GUARD	It'd be strange if we weren't.
K	I'm leaving.
FEMALE GUARD	No. You can't leave, you're under arrest.
K	What? Why?
MALE GUARD	That's not really our area.
K	What do you mean?
MALE GUARD	We just do this bit.
FEMALE GUARD	The guarding.
K	Then I'd like to see whosoever area it is.
FEMALE GUARD	We can't take this to them.

MRS BARROW tries to enter.

MRS BARROW	Oh, I'm sorry …

She backs out.

K	No, no, Mrs Barrow, / please …
MALE GUARD	What are you doing? You can't talk to her.

FEMALE GUARD	What's this, these ovular things?
K	They're for tying things up, I think. Why can't I talk to her?
FEMALE GUARD	Tying things up?
K	It used to be a stable; is it really that / important … ?
FEMALE GUARD	Make a note.
MALE GUARD	Sure. How do you spell 'Ovular'?
K	Don't write that down.
MALE GUARD	Because you say so?
K	Because it's not a word.
FEMALE GUARD	O-v-u-l-a-r.
MALE GUARD	Cheers.
K	Do you have a warrant?
MALE GUARD	'… tying up … horses'.
FEMALE GUARD	You're being very childish.
MALE GUARD	'… and dogs'.
FEMALE GUARD	The warrant doesn't matter.
MALE GUARD	I couldn't even say what they look like.
FEMALE GUARD	Me neither. We're just guards: we go where the department finds guilt. That's the Law.
K	I've never heard of a Law like that; I haven't done anything.
FEMALE GUARD	How do you know, if you've never heard of it?

MALE GUARD goes through K's clothes.

MALE GUARD	You think I can pull these off?
K	Put them down.
MALE GUARD	You won't need them. Guards get the clothes and the shoes, it's tradition.
FEMALE GUARD	And the underwear.
MALE GUARD	Underwear's 'clothes'.
K	You're not taking my underwear.

12

FEMALE GUARD I could fuck you right now.

MALE GUARD You're better off letting us. When we go, everything's taken to storage, and that place is a nightmare; you'll never get it back.

K But I can get it back from you?

MALE GUARD Get it back? Sure.

K Can I have a receipt?

FEMALE GUARD Of course. Mister ...?

K K.

FEMALE GUARD And how do I spell that?

K K.

FEMALE GUARD Yes ... ?

K Oh god. Very good. Very good. You nearly had me; it was the underwear thing, but apart from that ... Well, happy birthday to me. I suppose one of you is going to give me lapdance now; the other guy's going to come back with a stereo, is he? Unless you're actually ... Did they send you, from the bank?

FEMALE GUARD No. Ask them if you like.

K sees RABENSTEIN, KAMINER & KULLYCH.

Nice name, Josef K. Kind of lingers on the tongue.

K What are you doing here?

FEMALE GUARD Stay in your room, Josef K; maybe I'll come and join you.

MALE GUARD, FEMALE GUARD, and RABENSTEIN, KAMINER & KULLYCH leave.

K *unbreakfasted, still*

mayen best ee stay in room

all suren mistake, an soon arranged

keep ee blanken face; wary of shew im thought,
for ee watched all round neighbour windows still

latework

how ee found? mayen im spies be neighbours, all,
jaws a-pant

more now, up at glass like bastard aquarium

neutralface

im never banged up for thinken oom own head

strange im left alone

recent arrested, all distract of mind an worry, ee might bootlace im own life

serven right if ee dangling when they return

of course, no reason for ee innocent to do it

but war: im must do what ee enemy want least

perhaps, alone room, surround by witness staren neighbours, im all end from ceiling

that show em

MRS BARROW enters.

MRS BARROW	Mr K?
K	Hello?
MRS BARROW	They said it was all right just to bring you this.
K	Thank you, that's very kind.
MRS BARROW	It's no problem.
K	Are they still there?
MRS BARROW	Yes.
K	It's one thing to harass me, but bringing those three here just to humiliate me?
MRS BARROW	Maybe I should leave you to it —
K	No, please stay.
	I'm sorry for all the inconvenience.
MRS BARROW	What do you mean?
K	Them.
MRS BARROW	They're no bother.
K	They are to me; they're even trying to drag Rosa into this, whatever it is.
MRS BARROW	They picked the wrong one, if you ask me.
K	What do you mean?

MRS BARROW	Of the two of you, I'd say Coco has more to be embarrassed about.
K	Everyone uses a different name there.
MRS BARROW	If you're not embarrassed, there's no need to use a different name, is there? If they'd told me they were looking for some sort of impropriety, then I'd have said they're in the wrong flat.
K	She's not some whore, she's a bartender –
MRS BARROW	I have a reputation to maintain –
K	And how exactly does she damage it?
MRS BARROW	You must have heard the noises.
K	I haven't heard anything.
MRS BARROW	And she stays behind after work with … I don't know what you call people who go to clubs like that.
K	Customers.
MRS BARROW	I wouldn't know.
K	It's 'customers'; it's a bar.
MRS BARROW	Whatever you call them, people talk.
K	It doesn't stop you taking her money.
MRS BARROW	I'm just saying –
K	If you're worried about your reputation, then maybe you should throw me out. No one's come to arrest Rosa.
MRS BARROW	I was only trying to / tell you …
K	I know what you were trying to do –
MRS BARROW	Please, let's not fight, not over her.
	Should I offer them something?
K	God no; they've already had one breakfast off me.
MRS BARROW	No, I mean your colleagues.
K	Are they still here?

K sees RABENSTEIN, KAMINER & KULLYCH.

K	Get rid of them.

MRS BARROW I didn't know you didn't want / them here ...

K Just get them out; thank you.

MRS BARROW ushers RABENSTEIN, KAMINER & KULLYCH out, and leaves.

K *god dam crusted bitch*

attack ee young innocent, dam shrivelled sack

ee leap immediate latenight men's cocks conclusion

sneer an slander behind ee back, an take ee money
oom smilen face

maybe im Rosa discuss?

ee two alliance, confront, demand ee apology

no — mayen Rosa leave, never seen again

but still, im not allow slander oom saggy gossip
witch

worse than neighbours

oh yes, still stare oom windows

yes, hello all, welcome

watch an stare, an glass of wine for show

MALE GUARD and FEMALE GUARD enter.

FEMALE GUARD Josef K. The Comptroller wants you.

K I thought he'd gone.

MALE GUARD Why would he go? Come on.

FEMALE GUARD Wait, you can't see him like that, he'll have us flogged. Smarten yourself up; have some pride.

K Do you mind?

MALE GUARD Can't leave you alone; you might do anything.

FEMALE GUARD No, not that. You have a jacket? Black one? Not dark blue. Not charcoal.

K I don't have a good black jacket.

FEMALE GUARD A reasonable one, then. That'll do, quick, quick.

K *ee one second want to compose an waitwaitwait*
an settle, but not listen the slut, nor the idiot

16

> they taken her flat; fullen delicate unders an
> woman scent
>
> oom she let them?

MALE GUARD *and* FEMALE GUARD *take* K *to* ROSA'S *room.*

COMPTROLLER	Finally.
K	Where's Rosa?
COMPTROLLER	I know what you're thinking. I wouldn't do it. She'd snap you like a lolly stick.
K	I don't know what you're talking about.
COMPTROLLER	So, Mr K. I expect you're surprised by this morning's events.
K	Of course I'm surprised, I haven't done anything. I wouldn't say it caught me completely off-guard, though.
COMPTROLLER	No?
K	Well, not because … can I sit down?
COMPTROLLER	Tired?
K	What I mean is that, when you've been on this planet for thirty-five years, and had to make your way through it on your own, little things like this don't knock you off balance for long.
COMPTROLLER	But your mother's still alive?
K	There's clearly some mistake here; have you even looked at my ID?
COMPTROLLER	You think we don't know who you are?
K	I'm not sure I like what you're implying.
COMPTROLLER	You're claiming you're innocent?
K	Of course I am. Unlike your colleagues; I want their theft noted.
COMPTROLLER	Theft?
K	They took my clothes, and ate my breakfast.
COMPTROLLER	Everything belongs to the Court, Mr K.
K	This whole thing is a gross invasion of privacy; I may not know the legal wording, but I'm sure my friend Mr Goodspeed at the prosecutor's office will be delighted to help with that.

COMPTROLLER   You'd like to register a complaint?

K   I certainly would.

COMPTROLLER   All right.

K   Anything else you want while you're here? Fingerprints? Hair, blood, semen?

MRS BARROW *enters.*

MRS BARROW   Oh, excuse me ...

COMPTROLLER   Semen?

K   No, Mrs Barrow ...

MRS BARROW *leaves.*

COMPTROLLER   We can get all those from you at the station.

K   The station?

COMPTROLLER   Where else would you register a complaint?

K   I don't have time to go down to the station.

COMPTROLLER   It's on the record; I can't change it just because you say so. Do you often try this? My colleagues said you tried to stop them taking notes, too.

K   I tried to stop them looking like idiots.

COMPTROLLER   'Ovular'. That's not a word.

K   That's what I told them.

COMPTROLLER   Read that for me.

K   'Tying up dogs'.

COMPTROLLER   Now why did you bring that up?

K   I'd like to know of what I am accused. Are you the police? No one's even wearing a uniform.

COMPTROLLER   Whatever uniform we are, or are not, wearing has no bearing on how very serious your case is, Mr K. I can't tell you what you've been accused of, because I don't know if you have been accused. All I know is that you have been arrested.

K   Then I'd like to speak to someone who does know.

COMPTROLLER	I can't trouble the Higher Court about something like this. But you should take this seriously; smarten yourself up. If I might offer you a little advice: don't go on about how innocent you feel. You'd make a good impression, otherwise.
K	It's not that I feel innocent –
COMPTROLLER	You see? You should talk less. Everything you said could be inferred from your behaviour.
K	I see.
COMPTROLLER	That's better. Concise. I've informed you of the arrest, and noted your reaction; you probably want to head off to the bank now.
K	So I can just go?
COMPTROLLER	Of course.
K	Being under arrest doesn't seem that bad.
COMPTROLLER	No one ever said it was. Your colleagues can walk you there. I asked them here to make the whole transition as smooth as possible for you.

K sees RABENSTEIN, KAMINER & KULLYCH.

K	*how long stand oom three idiot mutes?*
	they no context
	im musten keep all quiet, unradar
	heh
	but who could better than silent fools to keep secrets?
	keepen close, finden work, keep oom busy
	im open eye keep
COMPTROLLER	Your friend Rosa's on the way.
K	Are you serious? We can't be in here.
COMPTROLLER	She wouldn't mind, would she?
K	Where's the key?
COMPTROLLER	I see.
K	The key?

COMPTROLLER leaves.

ROSA enters.

K	Rosa?
ROSA	Yes?
K	It's me; Josef. From next door.
ROSA	Yes, I know; hi.
K	Hi. Sorry, am I keeping you?
ROSA	I was just getting back in.
K	Sorry.

MRS BARROW enters.

ROSA	It's fine; don't worry / about it.
MRS BARROW	Good morning. Long night?
ROSA	Oh, you have no idea; I'm beat.
MRS BARROW	Mmm.
K	That's not ...
ROSA	OK. Good night Mrs Barrow, Josef; morning, rather.

MRS BARROW leaves.

K	Rosa, could I have a quick word?
ROSA	Can it wait 'til later?
K	I have to go to work ...
ROSA	A couple of minutes, then, but we've got to keep it down; she's gagging for an excuse to throw me out. Hang on, wait there; I need to change.
K	All right.

ROSA enters her room.

> *she probab tidy underwear an stockings, strewn*
> *all over*
>
> *im not embarrass of underwear; ee already seen,*
> *shoulden say no need*
>
> *too late now*

ROSA	Come in, then.
	You wanted a word?
K	It's a little embarrassing, so just to come out with it: your room was disturbed earlier on. Not by me, but I was at least partly responsible, and that's what I wanted to apologise. For.
ROSA	OK. So you didn't do it?
K	No.
ROSA	But it was your fault?
K	Partly.
ROSA	And how's that?
K	It really isn't that interesting.
ROSA	Shouldn't I be the judge of that? Well, I don't want to pry into your dirty secrets. If you say it's not interesting, fine: Josef K, I do grant a full, free and absolute pardon for any and all offenses you may have committed. Now go forth, and sin no more.
K	Are you angry?
ROSA	I'm just tired; please.
K	I don't want you to be angry with me.
ROSA	Well, maybe you shouldn't have come barging into my room ... did you touch my pictures?
K	It wasn't me, I swear; it must have been them.
ROSA	Who?
K	They brought three clerks to take me back to the bank.
ROSA	Who's 'they'?
K	I don't know; some sort of inquiry.
ROSA	An inquiry in my room? Because of you?
K	Yes.
ROSA	No.
K	Yes. You don't believe me?
ROSA	You don't seem the type; apart from the breaking and entering.

K   It was their idea; I didn't do anything.

ROSA   What do 'they' say you've done?

K   They didn't say.

ROSA   You must have done something.

K   No. The whole thing's ridiculous; I don't want to talk about it.

ROSA   Come on, while I'm still conscious. Give me the highlights.

K   OK, but you have to visualise everyone, it's complicated. I'm the
           Comptroller, here, he does all the questioning; '"Ovular". That's
           not a word'

ROSA   It isn't, is it?

K   That's what I told them. Then he asked me why I was bringing
           up dogs.

ROSA   You haven't got a dog.

K   That's ... do you want to be the Comptroller?

ROSA   Ok. I just talk about dogs, do I?

K   Mostly. There's a man and a woman over there; they said they
           were guards, but ... actually, I'm sure she was trying to ... you
           know. That she was interested in me.

ROSA   Of course she was; nothing more attractive than a criminal.

K   She did take my underwear.

ROSA   Did she pull your hair and run away as well?

K   You weren't there —

ROSA   Was he flirting with you, too?

K   There was something going on.

ROSA   If you say so.

K   Those three men, my colleagues, over there, probably fiddling
           with your pictures; fiddle, fiddle, fiddle.

ROSA   Creepy.

K   And all around us the bloody neighbours. People probably look
           in here all the time, don't they?

ROSA   So where are you?

22

K	I'm over here. Actually, I will be the Comptroller; do you want to be me?
ROSA	I was just getting into it.
K	Someone's got to be me.
ROSA	What about you?
K	I know what he did.
ROSA	You know what you did, too.
K	Yes, but the Comptroller did all the talking; I didn't say much.
ROSA	Could that be part of the problem?
K	You are not helping.
ROSA	All right, I'll be you. 'I haven't done anything. I'm innocent. Give me my pants back.'
K	So, I'm the Comptroller – actual me, not the me that you're playing –
ROSA	Thanks.
K	– and I'm over here.
ROSA	'There's clearly some mistake here.'
K	Good; and now, the guards call me – call you – in: 'Josef K.'
ROSA	I told you to keep it down.
K	I'm so sorry, I just got carried away.
ROSA	Sorry, Mrs Barrow. I bet she's scrambling for the bloody incident book –
K	I'll straighten it out, I promise; it's my fault.
ROSA	So you admit it, do you?
K	Don't start.
ROSA	She's going to throw me out, you know –
K	I won't let her; I'll protect you, I promise.

K kisses ROSA.

ROSA	No, come on; not now, just go.
K	I'm not going –

ROSA	Please.
K	– until you're all right.
ROSA	I am all right.
K	OK, but we need to come up with something to explain the noise. If we say I assaulted you, she'd believe that.
ROSA	Assaulted me?
K	Yes, you know. Assault. Why wouldn't she believe that?
ROSA	I'd have trouble.
K	I could assault you.
ROSA	Could you?
K	No, of course I wouldn't; but a single man, exuberant on his birthday …
ROSA	Happy birthday.
K	Thank you – and an attractive young woman who's just got in, it's early, they're alone in her room while everyone else is asleep … you could believe he might go a bit far.
ROSA	Josef; thank you, this … it's been interesting, but I'm just too tired for all this now; I've been up all night, and / it's just too much.
K	That's fine, I'll leave you to it; good night. Good morning, rather.
ROSA	Bye.

ROSA *leaves.*

K	*progress*
	invite, an talk
	an Rosa not some innocent, ee know effect of im *watchen ready for bed*
	an let im kiss
	progress
	if ee not be surround by neighbours all a-stare *again –*
	yes, hello

24

not a wave

if ee not surround an waited by three idiot mute

Rosa Rosalita Rosamunda

oom kiss ee hang on perfume lips still

K arrives at the bank.

K   *work an safe*

ee final settle, oom calm, control, safen interrupt

surround ee familiar noise an rhythm comfort

hello papers, distant drones

musten sure ee droneworkers knowen nothing oom morning nonsense

an keepen watch ee hovering mutes

ee office settle

calm

oom only caught unready at home

if ee assault by dam officers at work, then oom full prepared

ee invasion untroubled, answer all im questions, an turn ee bastards away

Voice   Good morning. This is a message for Josef K. The preliminary inquiry into your case has now been opened, and this message contains all the information you need to obtain a full and satisfactory investigation.

Your trial is important to us. Hearings will take place on a given day of every week. This day has been personally tailored to your individual requirements, to minimise inconvenience to your personal and professional life, and to allow maximum enjoyment of the duration. Your day is —

Sunday.

Your first hearing will take place at the next occurrence of your allocated hearing day, and will continue weekly until the conclusion of your case. Thank —

pulls out the answerphone tape; KYLE enters.

KYLE	Bad news?
K	What? No, it's nothing; tape's just broken. What's up?
KYLE	I thought you weren't in today.
K	What? Why?
KYLE	I don't know; it's just what everyone was saying.
K	Everyone.
KYLE	You know; people.
K	Right; bit of a household emergency.
KYLE	You too? My pipes burst; havoc in the cellar.
K	No.
KYLE	Every label soaked off; not a clue what's actually in there. And insurance? Not a hope. 'The wine's undamaged'. You OK?
K	Yes.
KYLE	Sure?
K	I'm fine.
KYLE	All right, but let me know if I can help.
K	With what?
KYLE	Whatever.
K	All right.
KYLE	Listen, sorry for the fire drill, but we've really got to lock down the Welsers today.
K	Them. Don't worry, I'm on it.
KYLE	Great. Me too.
K	You don't need to / worry about …
KYLE	Actually, I sort of do; come down from above.
K	There's barely enough for one.
KYLE	I know that, and you know that, but they want someone to cover.
K	God's sake, Kyle, it's a favour for the board; it's all basically below the bar anyway —

KYLE	I'm sure your domestic wasn't your fault, but the whole damned Welser lot are coming in this afternoon, and if we lose them just because there's no one else in the loop, there's going to be scalpings. I'm not going to get under your feet; it'll be fun.
K	Fun.
KYLE	Fun. You said it, barely any work, plenty of credit for all. Happy days.
K	All right. We'll talk about it later. Something else?
KYLE	Just … what are you doing on Sunday morning?
K	This Sunday?
KYLE	Yeah. I'm having sort of a little party; a brunch thing, on the boat.
K	Christ, who died and left you enough for a boat?
KYLE	My dad.
K	Right, yes. Sorry.
KYLE	Anyway. It's just going to be a little pow wow, you know: few of the other VPs, some guys from the council; that prosecutor, Goodspeed, he's coming. Rosa's going to be there.
K	What, my Rosa?
KYLE	Is she your Rosa?
K	Not 'my Rosa'; the Rosa from my building.
KYLE	That's the one; told her you might be there. So, you coming?
K	I really would, but there's a thing.
KYLE	On a Sunday morning? What sort of thing?
K	It's a personal … well, not personal, exactly –
KYLE	All right. We'll be there all day, come along after.
K	I think it might be quite a long thing.
KYLE	Offer's there. Listen, I've got to get back; it's a bloodbath out there.
K	What is?

KYLE	Dawn raid on DMJ; probably the Japanese.
K	Of course it is, I wrote that up last quarter.
KYLE	Clever you. You're in for the day now?
K	Yes.
KYLE	Right. Happy birthday.

KYLE *leaves.*

K   they worken quick

im once unready caught at home

not again

ee Court im every week demand?

steel im to task, now: first hearing attend, then ee
certain be the last

ee musten proclaim im innocent, an im put all
facts before ee judge, im wrong arrest, an all be done

im musten end oom whole trial immediate

K *arrives at the courtroom.*

MAGISTRATE	You were supposed to be here an hour and five minutes ago.
	You were supposed to be here an hour and five minutes ago.
K	I may have arrived late, but I'm here now.

Wild applause.

MAGISTRATE	Given how late you are, I'm no longer required to examine you. Nevertheless, I think we should continue with the proceedings; we've lost enough time already.
K	How kind … is it 'Your honour'? I only know how to address actual officials, you see.

Laughter and applause.

MAGISTRATE	That sort of thing won't help. So, you're a decorator.
K	No, I'm an Associate Vice President at a major bank.
	That explains it; if you're looking for some decorator, then you really have arrested the wrong man.
MAGISTRATE	The Court doesn't make mistakes, Mr K. It seeks out guilt.

K   But you think I'm this decorator. And whoever he is, aren't both of us innocent until proven guilty as well? Are you going to hang us just for defending ourselves?

MAGISTRATE   This Court will not decide anything of the sort –

K   Then take me to the Court that will.

MAGISTRATE   Defendants can't simply progress to the Higher Court, Mr K; this is only the first hearing, to / decide what …

K   I'm not prepared to waste any more of my time on this, Your Honour, I'm an executive whose time is a valuable commodity; but since I'm here, I'd like certain things put on the record. To be concise, I have done nothing wrong; if I had any doubt at all, I'd be ashamed to have anyone know that I was recently – quote, unquote – arrested. Let me tell you a little about how that occurred.

           You couldn't dream up a more brazen example of how power corrupts than my two guards. Who were they? They had no badges, no warrants, nothing; they certainly had no power to demand bribes, commandeer my clothes, eat my breakfast, drag me into my neighbour's flat, that they'd clearly broken into, and ineptly interrogate me. Maybe they thought I was this decorator you've been looking for.

           Let me be clear that I'm not here out of self-interest, but I'd like to use my case as an example of what goes on in the name of this Court. If it's happened to me, then it's happened to others, and it'll happen again unless someone with some mettle makes a stand.

           So I'm here to put an end to this, once and for all. Let me assure you that if I had even a shred of doubt, I'd be on my knees begging for mercy; so, if anyone has a single piece of evidence against me, then show us all, and judge me right now.

The Court officials display a series of tattoos.

K   Oh, Your Honour, if you're flagging so much that you need your cronies' help, just say so; there's no need for any of this nonsense.

           Nothing? Then I think we can say that we all know the truth: that this has been a witch hunt.

CHASTITY and the STUDENT are having sex in the middle of the Court room, watched by the officials.

K   Interesting. Is this how desperate you are? It's pathetic. If you think this little man ploughing away is going to throw me off, then you've underestimated me.

STUDENT   I'm trying to concentrate.

Wild laughter and applause.

MAGISTRATE   Mr K, the Court is only interested in what you have to tell us; if you're leaving, I should tell you you're abandoning all the advantages an accused man has. The next hearing isn't conducted on such favourable terms.

K   Conduct it on whatever terms you like; I won't be there. If the Higher Court wants me, it knows where to find me. I've said everything I need to say, and if you're going to hang me, you'll have to come and get me.

K leaves the courtroom.

K   not quite as expect

               not unsuccess, sure

               im maken clear ee serious an should untrifled

               but still they think im guilt

KYLE enters.

KYLE   I'm not saying it's great practice, but it's not unethical.

K   All right.

KYLE   Gamesmanship, yes, but it's legitimate; if they're not going to do their own due diligence, then fair enough. It's not our responsibility to do their job for them, is it?

K   It's a good point.

KYLE   You all right?

K   Fine.

KYLE   You know there's someone here for you, don't you?

K   What? Can you tell them I'm / busy ... ?

ALBERT enters.

ALBERT   Josef, I'm sorry to intrude.

30

K	Never mind. Hello Uncle, very good to see you. How can I help?

KYLE *leaves.*

ALBERT	This is your office? You've done well.
K	Thank you; a little luck and a lot of hard work. How's my mother?
ALBERT	She's fine.
K	Good. Albert, I'm sorry, but you really should have made an appointment –
ALBERT	I've heard some rumours, and I'd like you to tell me they're not true.
K	All right. They're not true.
ALBERT	No?
K	I've no idea what you're talking about, so it's / hard to say.
ALBERT	The rumours we've heard are about your being arrested.
K	Keep it down, please. How did you hear about this?
ALBERT	So it is true?
K	Yes, it's true, in a way, but it's nothing to worry about. Now what can I do for you?
ALBERT	I came here to help you.
K	Is that it? That's kind, but I think I have it all in hand. It's good to see you, but I'm right in the middle –
ALBERT	Trials like this don't just happen; whatever they told you, this has been a long time coming, they build up, they accumulate. You should have talked to me months ago.
K	I didn't know about it months ago.
ALBERT	You just found out and you've come in to work?
K	Will you please keep it down?
ALBERT	For god's sake, pull yourself together, boy. How can you just sit there with a trial snapping at your bloody heels? You need help. Have you seen what they can do?
K	Some.

ALBERT	And you still think your best course of action is ignoring it? Do you?
K	No. All right; I'm listening.
ALBERT	Good. Then we should go to see Mrs Grace; she'll know what to do next.
K	Mrs Grace the lawyer?
ALBERT	Yes, of course the lawyer. She'll need all the papers from whoever you have now.
K	I didn't know you could get a lawyer for this kind of thing.
ALBERT	You don't have one?
K	No.
ALBERT	I should have come sooner; you need to start taking this seriously. We've lost enough time already; we should go, right now.
K	All right.
ALBERT	Good. Is that what you're wearing?
K	Yes.
ALBERT	You don't have a better jacket?

KYLE *enters.*

KYLE	Afternoon.
ALBERT	Good afternoon. Josef, come on.
KYLE	Are you off?
K	I have to go out. Personal thing.
KYLE	If you have to. And the Welser stuff?
K	Not now, no.
KYLE	All right; I'll go through it.
K	It's a bit arcane –
KYLE	This all of it?
K	Basically –
ALBERT	We have to go now.
K	Just wait; there's some cousin –

32

KYLE	It's fine, I've got it.
K	This has to go well.
ALBERT	Josef.
K	I mean it.
KYLE	The transition will be as smooth as possible.

K and ALBERT leave.

K	*ee musten calm*
	oom Court they never believe im innocent
	ee pointless protest oom mistaken wrong man
	logic say ee Court game musten play
	defend ee accusation, refute im argument an ee prove im innocent oom Court
	yes
	im uncle an ee lawyer be best idea

K and ALBERT arrive at GRACE'S offices.

ALBERT	Hello? Open up, come on.
CHERRY	Mrs Grace is ill.
ALBERT	Who the hell are you? Open the damned door.
CHERRY	She's ill.
K	Let's just go; we can come back / some other …
ALBERT	I'm not going to be put off by some girl.
CHERRY	Oh my god. Hi Josef.
K	Hello.
CHERRY	Are you coming in?
K	Yes.
CHERRY	Oh my god. OK; great, hang on, wait there.
ALBERT	I knew this would happen. Stay away.
CHERRY	Hi.
K	Hello.
ALBERT	Keep back, please.

CHERRY	Can I just get in quickly?
ALBERT	We're in a hurry; come on.
CHERRY	I'll show you the way.
ALBERT	I remember the way.
CHERRY	How long are you here for?
ALBERT	Don't talk to her.
K	I don't know.
ALBERT	Don't talk to her.
CHERRY	It's really nice to meet you.
K	It's nice to meet you, too.
CHERRY	Do you need anything?
K	What do you / mean?
ALBERT	We're not here for her. Come on.
CHERRY	No, wait —
ALBERT	Mrs Grace?

GRACE and FAYE are doing a jigsaw.

GRACE	Christ, Cheryl, I told you no visitors.
ALBERT	Grace?
FAYE	I thought you said you weren't expecting anyone.
GRACE	I'm not.
FAYE	There's a queue.
GRACE	Yes, hello, thank you for coming, but I'm afraid my books are burstingly full, so you will need to find alternative representation at this time, thank you so much for your interest.
ALBERT	It's Albert …
GRACE	Albert; good god, how good to see you. Come in, come in.
FAYE	They can come back, can't they?
ALBERT	It's good of you to see us.
GRACE	Of course I'd see you. Do you need anything?

ALBERT	No, we're fine.
CHERRY	Josef, can I get you anything?
ALBERT	Miss, please. We need to talk in private.
GRACE	She's not going to spill your secrets.
ALBERT	It's not my secrets I'm worried about.
CHERRY	Will you say goodbye before you go?
GRACE	Cheryl.

CHERRY leaves.

FAYE	How long are you going to be?
GRACE	As long as it takes. Go on.

FAYE leaves.

GRACE	So, what brings you out here in such a panic after all these years?
ALBERT	This is my nephew, Josef K.
GRACE	Yes, I know; I'd assumed he was taller. I wondered if our paths would cross, and I see providence has … provided.
K	More my uncle than providence.
GRACE	Very good. Yes, you'll do well. I'm not as young as I was, and my health may not last such an involved trial, but if that turns out to be the case, at least yours offers a worthy obstacle on which to fail. There.
K	How do you know about my trial?
GRACE	I am frighteningly good at my job. I pick up details here and there in conversation that would elude a milder brain, and I recall them when the moment arises; not so hard when they involve the nephew of an old friend.
K	Do you always put so much faith in rumours?
GRACE	If I trust their source.
ALBERT	Mrs Grace, we would be very grateful for your help.
K	Yes.

GRACE	Good. We must get moving, we've lost enough time already. I should begin by saying that your case seems hopeless –
K	All right –
GRACE	– but that I've already won, or come excruciatingly close to winning, many trials that looked even more desperate. I keep a list of them for inspiration.
K	Can I see it?
GRACE	By no means. Proceedings aren't public, you know; they can be made public, but I can't remember the last time the Court made such a request, can you Albert?
ALBERT	I can't recall –
GRACE	– which of course means that all case records, including your own, are inaccessible.
K	You can't request my case records?
GRACE	If I could, Mr K, I wouldn't have needed to develop such voluminous skill. You can't request them either, which is exactly why your petition must be so comprehensive: we're looking for anything they could use against you, so you need to think back over your entire life and document every potential transgression. They like narrative, and they like context, so you should take each incident and describe the surrounding events to the fullest of your memory, place them within the story of your life, explain why you enacted your response in the manner outlined in the previous, and conclude by saying whether, with the benefit of hindsight, you would act differently in the now-present.
K	My entire life? And that'll help?
GRACE	There's an old saying: 'a petition paints a thousand words'.
K	Is there?
GRACE	But a good petition will be much longer, of course. Since the charge is entirely unknowable, we must cover the widest ground possible with the first submission. We can only devise a fully pertinent petition later, when more details emerge, and we know which of those to address. Albert, I'll expedite discovery

as best I can, starting tomorrow with a three-pronged assault:
all officials are creatures of habit, and I'm certain to encounter
his particular Magistrate at lunch, where I'll engage him 1)
on general issues of the day, before working the conversation
around to 2) the specifics of his case. The afternoon I will spend
3) profitably stationed by the door to the courtroom, gleaning
what details I may from the traffic thereabouts.

K	Why don't you just go in?
GRACE	Please don't interrupt while I'm speaking about you in the third person. The Court doesn't allow lawyers for the defence, which means I need to work through other means. It's rarely a problem; I don't know if you noticed, but I'm extremely likeable.
K	Are you seriously suggesting I retain a lawyer who can't go into a courtroom?
ALBERT	She's very skilled.
GRACE	He's right. I am. You should trust me implicitly. No doubt you've already learnt that the lowest and most desperate levels of the Court can be easily swayed by even the smallest of bribes; I should warn you that other, less enjoyable, lawyers will try to persuade you to exploit this situation. I would advise you to resist them: in the short term, it might seem that they're getting positive results, which they'll parade around to the envy of your cohorts; ultimately, though, that sort of thing will do irreparable damage to your case. The only truly useful thing is personal contact with higher officials.
ALBERT	Higher officials of the lower courts, of course.
GRACE	Oh yes, not the higher officials *per se*; can you imagine? Let me be nakedly frank with you: I can't offer him access to the Higher Court, and neither can anyone else, whatever they say. The prudent lawyer concerns herself with those higher echelons of the lower Court who can have a direct influence on those cases that interest her. I don't want to bang my own trumpet, but I'm fortunate enough to be visited by many such officials, and they'll frequently offer clear, or easily interpreted, information, as well as discussing the progress of their recent trials, which may touch on issues relevant to his case, and I will not be

looking their gift horses anywhere. Of course, they'll quite often return to their offices and declare the exact opposite, perhaps even more severely, so we can't trust them too much. But, as you know, there's no way to protect against this eventuality: a private conversation –

ALBERT	– is a private conversation –
GRACE	– is a private conversation, exactly, with no public consequences.
ALBERT	But presumably none of this is philanthropy.
GRACE	Of course not.
ALBERT	They depend on lawyers too, it's a two-way horse.
GRACE	Give and take, yes, and this is the problem: the officials have no contact with the man on the street.
ALBERT	Exactly.
GRACE	They can cope perfectly well with these run-of-the-mill cases that just roll along on their own, gathering no moss, but when something more complex crops up –
ALBERT	– or even something very simple –
GRACE	– very true, yes, and because they're hemmed in by the Law, they don't understand the simple human engagement on the issues. And how many eggs do they have in their basket then?
ALBERT	Exactly, and I've always said this is the trouble with engaging only at the micro level.
GRACE	They'll never have the chance to learn –
ALBERT	– there's no perspective, there's no sense of the macro, is / there?
GRACE	– by studying – yes, exactly – the individual stages of a trial, because their involvement is limited to the tiny sliver of action that's laid before them.
ALBERT	And they stamp it all of course, but there's no perspective.
GRACE	It's the context –
ALBERT	– context, yes
GRACE	– that they're missing. It's Peters versus Lemonvan.

ALBERT   Exactly.

GRACE   It's focusing on the gun and ignoring the wife in the cupboard;
           it's not having that association with the defendant himself.
           While the defence is in constant contact with the accused, right
           to the end.

An enormous noise; GRACE and ALBERT recede from K.

GRACE   So, we have some leverage there; for his part, though,
           he needs to be kept on a short leash.

ALBERT   I agree.

GRACE   Because every defendant goes charging in there with his
           great big brush, slapping his whitewash around, and he's
           already too far gone to allow that kind of distraction
           from the main thrust of the case.

ALBERT   Agreed.

GRACE   You accept the bowl as you find it. And even if he
           could change the smallest detail, which is basically just
           an absurd superstition, but even if he could, it'd only
           help the future and waste time in the here now
           when he should be worrying about the whole,
           colossal squid being interconnected, and the
           beast will put out a tentacle somewhere
           else, while he's busy chopping the ground
           away from under his feet.

ALBERT   The squid is the priority, then?

GRACE   The squid, yes, but more important than
           that is preliminary discussions with the
           hand that feeds you.

ALBERT   Tentacles at lunch tomorrow?

GRACE   And then we begin the long process of
           approaching the relevant officials; I

CHERRY   Hi Josef.   should say that, sometimes, it'll seem
                                          totally hopeless, and that the only

K   Hello. Was that you?   trials that are going well are those
                                          that were destined to go well

39

CHERRY	Was what me?

Maybe. I thought you might like an excuse to get out of there.

from the start, and that perhaps all our work isn't having as much of an effect as we'd like; I can only say that we are in a good …

K	You could have knocked.
CHERRY	Would you have come?
K	Of course.
CHERRY	I'm Cherry.
K	Hello, Cherry.
CHERRY	Hi. It's actually you.
K	Yes.
CHERRY	How's it going?
K	How's what going?
CHERRY	What do you think? The trial; I've been following it for ages. Everyone's just heard rumours.
K	What rumours?
CHERRY	All sorts of things.
K	Like?
CHERRY	Like that interesting people get interesting cases.
K	Really? So, in your expert opinion, what do you think I should do?
CHERRY	I think you've got to confess.

CHERRY notices BLOCK.

CHERRY	Get back to work. He's curious about you. Never mind about him, he's no one. She'll call if there's any news. Back to work.

BLOCK leaves.

K	Who is that?
CHERRY	Don't worry about him, he won't be around long. Do you need help? I could go with you, I know loads of places they'd never look for us.

K	I'm not sure that's a good idea.
CHERRY	I thought you didn't care about the Law.
K	I don't; the Law seems to have a strong interest in me.
CHERRY	They'd never find out; not from me, anyway.
K	They'd find out.
CHERRY	But how could they, if we were miles way, all alone, in a cottage out on the moor, by a roaring fire …?
	What's wrong? It's Rosa, isn't it?
K	How do you know about Rosa?
CHERRY	I know all sorts of things. So it's true? You two?
K	We're not together.
CHERRY	But you're with someone?
K	Sort of.
CHERRY	Who is it? Come on, you can tell me.

CHERRY finds TIFFANY's card in K's pocket.

CHERRY	Who's this? Who's Tiffany?
K	She's a friend.
CHERRY	I don't know her; how long have you been seeing her?
K	A while.
CHERRY	What does she do?
K	She dances, sometimes.
CHERRY	I can dance.
	Do you love her?
K	It's not like that.
CHERRY	When you go and see her, do you get to stay the night? You can have more than that, if you want.
	Not your type?
K	You're perfect.
CHERRY	No, I'm a freak.
	People like you and me don't want perfect, do we?

K	What else have you heard?
CHERRY	Here I am, waiting for you, and you're still thinking about your trial.
K	No one else is going to take care of it.
CHERRY	I'll take care of you.
K	You don't know me.
CHERRY	I know you. I could fuck you right now.

CHERRY *and* K *fail to have sex.*

CHERRY	You don't want to?
K	the little deformity lusten for him right away
	an ee limp lie, mind oom Rosa fixed
	snow down on still shape dog on motorroad
	still her taste on ee lips
CHERRY	Josef?
K	It's not that.
CHERRY	Next time, then; come whenever you want. You belong to me now.

ALBERT *enters.*

ALBERT	You. Get away from him.
CHERRY	We're together; tell him.
ALBERT	You're a stupid little girl. Crawl back to your damned hole.

CHERRY *leaves.*

ALBERT	Is this where you went? I come back here after years, to persuade an old friend to help you, and you crawl off to screw some little vampire?

ALBERT *recedes from* K.

ALBERT	I was so embarrassed. I brought you here to try to help you, I've called in favours left, right and centre to line up everything for your defence, and this is how seriously you take it? She's a busy woman, she's not going to go through it all again. We had to just sit there, pretending we hadn't noticed you'd just wandered off.

Of course I knew where you were, I saw you eyeing up that little tart from the second we came in, but I didn't think you'd just rush off to wet your wick like that.

    You could have saved yourself a lot of work, she was all ready to do most of it for you; you'll need to spend a lot of time on that petition now. She was talking about having a notary assigned to you, to conduct the interviews, type it all up, and then all you'd have to do is sign off on the transcript. That's

K   *ee oom so tired*   all on your shoulders now, so I suggest you get started immediately. Everything has to *ee eyes like sawdust* be documented, you understand? If they catch you in an omission or, god *oom whole dam thing* forbid, some kind of untruth, then *suck all ee energy* the whole thing will be a waste *mayen sleep, be calm* and your main line of defence *still too much im work* will just collapse …

K arrives at the bank.

KYLE	Where have you been?
K	I had to go out.
KYLE	All day? I'm about to go home.
K	Night, then.
KYLE	You threw me under the bus with the Welsers.
K	I'm sure you managed.
KYLE	I bluffed it; would've gone a lot better if we'd talked it over. You think you'll be able to squeeze us in next time?

The sound of flogging.

K	What is that?
KYLE	What's what?
	Is there some reason you don't want this to go well?
K	Of course there isn't.

KYLE   Good. So next time, we'll all sit round a table together, we'll talk it through, they'll be impressed with your insight, they'll sign and we decide how to spend our two percent. Right?

K   Don't worry about me.

KYLE   I do worry. I worry a lot. I'm not going to take this to anyone at the moment, ok, but it's not my job to carry dead weight.

K   I wouldn't have thought you'd mind working on my biggest clients.

KYLE   They're not your clients; they're the bank's clients, and I'm just doing my job, like you should be. You should go home; get some sleep.

KYLE leaves; RABENSTEIN, KAMINER & KULLYCH hover.

K   *dam thief bastard*

       know im about ee arrest?

       suren no

       but still, ee desperate claws on weakness

       im be worth an eye kept on

       ee musten trial focus

       mayen Cherry right; an ee confess, it all go away

       but how confess? ee nothing done

       if en Court want proof of Josef innocent, then oom show proof

Phone rings.

K   Leave it.

       ee lawyer mayen right

       im musten petition, an document ee life

       ee full life, all decision, leaven nothing to imagine

       list all oom events, an why ee act as ee do

       an would ee different now?

       an reasons for all

       eliminate ee all ambiguum, all doubten motive, maken clear all misunderstood

> if *ee* all explain, no room for suspect
>
> if *ee* all explain, then *ee musten* be free

Phone stops; the sound of flogging.

K   What is that?

> *begin*
>
> *where ee start? ee first remember?*
>
> *write ee down*
>
> *four years, ee hit oom girl Megan in playground*
>
> *ee weeping cry, an teacher see, oom smack*
>
> 'boys do not hit girls'
>
> *but she hit first*
>
> *no, not hit; she laughen with friends an try im kiss*
>
> *im provoked, so retaliate; not guilt*
>
> *good*
>
> *musten make official, ee all document*

K   One of you, take this to Mrs Grace.

The sound of flogging.

K   What is that?

K sees MALE GUARD, FEMALE GUARD and FLOGGER.

K   Jesus —

MALE GUARD Sir. Thank god, tell them it's all / a mistake.

K   What? Who are you, what are you doing here?

FEMALE GUARD Don't say anything; it's a trick.

MALE GUARD You complained about us to the Magistrate; you told them all we asked you for bribes.

K   You arrested me.

FEMALE GUARD Of course we did.

MALE GUARD Now he's going to flog us.

K   What, because of me?

MALE GUARD You said we stole your breakfast.

K	You did; and my clothes.
MALE GUARD	Oh, here it comes.
K	You did. Those are mine, aren't they?
MALE GUARD	It's tradition.
FEMALE GUARD	Please, if you knew how little we make doing / this, you'd
K	How little you / make?
FEMALE GUARD	He has a family to look after, I was saving up to get married –
K	Oh well, in that case –
MALE GUARD	I was going to be a flogger soon.
FEMALE GUARD	How can I start a family with this on my record?
MALE GUARD	You of all people should know that record's permanent.
K	You're the ones who assaulted me in my own room, who dragged me into my neighbour's flat, who took my bloody shoes. And I'm sorry if you're being punished for it, but I only told them exactly what you did.
MALE GUARD	And you think we deserve this?
K	I didn't ask for you to be flogged.
FLOGGER	They're lying; he doesn't have the discipline to be a flogger. Strip.
MALE GUARD	I'm not –
FLOGGER	Can't turn down a free breakfast, can you?
K	Let's just talk about this: if you leave now, who's to say that you didn't flog them? I could make it –
FLOGGER	My orders come from the Higher Court. I have my standards.
K	They were just following orders; if you had someone from the Higher Court here, I'd pay you to beat him harder.
FLOGGER	I can't be bought.
K	I wasn't trying to / buy you.
FEMALE GUARD	Please, I should be punished, you're right, someone should punish me. Couldn't you do it instead? Josef.

FLOGGER beats MALE GUARD *and* FEMALE GUARD.

K leaves; he sees KYLE *and* RABENSTEIN, KAMINER *&* KULLYCH.

K	It's me. It is me; it's fine. It's just a dog down in the courtyard. The noise. I heard a noise, you probably did too, so I had a look and it was a dog. Down there. Roaming around. Feral, probably.
	For god's sake, stop standing there. Clean out that storeroom, will you? Just do it; I can't stand this filth any longer. Get it out of there. We're drowning; we're drowning in filth.

Phone rings.

K	thirteen
	ee an friend, im both spy oom sixteen sister en shower
	of course im embarrassed to think
	yes, your honour, of course ee shame
	but ee child
	no worse, ee teenage, all over hormones
	who among us etcetera?

Phone stops.

K arrives at the courtroom.

CHASTITY	You here for the Court? There's no session today.
K	Why not? It's Sunday.
CHASTITY	Do I look like a lawyer?
K	No one does.
	That was you, wasn't it? At my hearing? With that …
CHASTITY	He's some law student. Not my choice. They know what they can get away with.
K	They do. Josef.
CHASTITY	I know. Chastity.
K	Ha. Sorry.
CHASTITY	I liked your speech.
K	Thank you.

CHASTITY	What I heard, anyway; he gets loud. You sounded like you wanted a revolution.
K	No, I've given up on that; I've enough to worry about. But if you need help …
CHASTITY	What, you'll help me?
K	If I can.
CHASTITY	Get me out of here. Take me away.
K	Take you away? You're married.
CHASTITY	Married? I woke up the other night with the Magistrate watching me in bed, and my husband lying next to me. He sends me underwear. That student does whatever he wants to me; no one cares I'm married.
	You going to help?
K	I'll do what I can.
CHASTITY	All right.
K	Can I look around?
CHASTITY	Course.

K looks at the law books, stuffed with pornographic photos.

K	So there is no Law, there's just this.
CHASTITY	There's Law.

K finds some photos of CHASTITY.

CHASTITY	He likes his camera. Sometimes, when he's pounding away, he goes ugh, and I imagine he's dying. He coughs, my back's wet, and this time it's blood. He grabs his chest and stares at me; there's blood coming of out his eyes and his ears. You could do that to him, couldn't you?
K	No.
CHASTITY	You said you'd help.
K	Not like that.
CHASTITY	Take some. I saw how you looked at me, in the courtroom; prefer you to those old men. I can be with you, if you get me out of here. I can help you.

K   All right.

CHASTITY   I could fuck you right now.

CHASTITY sees the STUDENT.

CHASTITY   He's watching.

K   Where?

CHASTITY   He's filth.

K   No, stay here.

CHASTITY   I have to go.

K   Why?

CHASTITY   I'll get away as soon as I can. You can do what you want to me.

STUDENT   You. What are you doing here?

K   I had a hearing.

STUDENT   There's no session today.

K   I can see that.

STUDENT   Don't let us keep you.

K   I don't think she wants to go.

STUDENT   I told them not to let him run around off his leash.

CHASTITY   I couldn't get rid of him.

K   Get off her.

CHASTITY   He's crazy.

K   She's staying with me.

CHASTITY   They should lock him up.

STUDENT   I'm taking her. Stop me.

CHASTITY   Don't worry about him, he won't last long.

STUDENT   Put your tongue out.

K   Get away from her.

STUDENT   Further; good.

K   What about what you said?

CHASTITY   I don't know what he's talking about. You stay away; I mean it.

The STUDENT carries CHASTITY away; K follows them.

K	oo why not take ee away, her all voluptuum, an supple, an take her to be oom Josef alone?
	an Rosa?
	im her lose, for all?
	no — ee saven this one, an Rosa see im strength
	ee see im hero

K sees MRS GRACE.

K	Mrs Grace?
GRACE	Josef, hello. Very committed, I see; bravo.
K	Are you here on my case?
GRACE	Always.
K	And what's the news? Did you get my papers?
GRACE	No news; that's not exactly how it works. But things are progressing nicely.
K	Are they?
GRACE	Everything's

moving

apace

K enters the Information Office, with a queue of defendants.

ASSISTANT	Good afternoon.
INFO. OFFICER	Afternoon.
DEFENDANT	There's a queue.
K	For what?
ASSISTANT	Can we help?
DEFENDANT	Hey. There's a queue.
K	I'm just looking for someone …
ASSISTANT	You have the search forms?
K	I was just looking …
ASSISTANT	Facially? No problem; just fill this one in —

DEFENDANT	I've been here for hours.
INFO. OFFICER	Josef K.
ASSISTANT	Him? You're Josef K? But there's no session today.
INFO. OFFICER	Did you not get the message?
K	My telephone's not working.
ASSISTANT	Ah. Could you fill that in as well, then? Thank you.
INFO. OFFICER	Who is it? This person you're looking for.
K	There was a cleaner, downstairs. Some student took her.
INFO. OFFICER	Chastity. She'll be with the Magistrate now.
ASSISTANT	You won't need that, then; but do keep a copy, for your records. And initial.
INFO. OFFICER	Since you're here, how can we assist? We are at your disposal.
DEFENDANT	Can you please hurry it up?
K	I can just ask you?
ASSISTANT	Of course; do write them down as we go, though.
K	Yes, of course. All right. What are they doing?
INFO. OFFICER	Waiting to research their cases.
DEFENDANT	For hours.

K sees BLOCK.

K	Who's that? Stop him.
DEFENDANT	You stop him.
ASSISTANT	We can't interfere.
DEFENDANT	Are you going, then?
K	No. What happened to my hearings? It's Sunday.
ASSISTANT	'Conduct it on whatever terms you like; I won't be there. I've said everything I need to say.'
INFO. OFFICER	That is what you said, isn't it?
K	Maybe, in the heat of the moment –
INFO. OFFICER	The Court only assembles at your demand, Mr K; as such, the hearings are being conducted without you.

K	Surely I'm allowed to defend myself?
INFO. OFFICER	Of course; Reinstatement Of Hearings?
ASSISTANT	Here we go.
INFO. OFFICER	Your magistrate will need to sign as well.
K	I don't know who he is.
INFO. OFFICER	Oh, we can easily find that out.
ASSISTANT	You have the search forms?
K	You took them back.
ASSISTANT	I don't have any more. Next time, then.
INFO. OFFICER	Your best defence is your petition, in any case. Have you been working on it?
K	Yes, my lawyer has it.
ASSISTANT	Good. And have you given notice that you have a lawyer?
K	I thought lawyers weren't allowed.
ASSISTANT	You don't want them to find out you've been hiding one. You'll need this one as well then, please.
INFO. OFFICER	If that's all … ?
K	*seven*

> *make piss on other boy's shoes an tell teacher he*
> *done wet himself in front of class.*

> *what ee expect? im limp weak, an hair smell off,*
> *an im always talk. if ee not do it, some other.*

ASSISTANT:	Mr K?
K	There has been a mistake.
INFO. OFFICER	I don't think so.
K	I'm telling you there has.
INFO. OFFICER	All right. And what was nature of this mistake?
K	I'm under arrest.
INFO. OFFICER	Yes.
K	I shouldn't be under arrest.

ASSISTANT	Oh.
INFO. OFFICER	I'm afraid that's not our area; we deal with issues that arise during the process of the trial, and since yours has already started —
K	Then whose area is it? Let me talk to them.
INFO. OFFICER	I can't just go putting you in touch with the Higher Court.
ASSISTANT	Why don't you tell us what happened?
K	I was lying in bed, and the Comptroller came in from Rosa's room —
INFO. OFFICER	Why does your flat have a door to Rosa's room?
K	I didn't build it. Two guards came in and told me I'm under arrest, while they stole my underwear and ate my breakfast. Then they broke into my neighbour's flat, dragged me in there to be interrogated in front of three clerks that they brought there solely for the purpose, started talking about my mother, and then sent me off to work without telling me why any of it happened in the first place.
INFO. OFFICER	And your complaint?
K	My complaint?
DEFENDANT	Come on, you've had your turn —
K	I am not done —
ASSISTANT	Don't touch him.
INFO. OFFICER	You shouldn't really do that.
ASSISTANT	You both need to sign this, now.
K	He started it.
ASSISTANT	The price of fame. Here, please. And here. You too.
INFO. OFFICER	Is there something else we can help you with?
ASSISTANT	There's your copy …
K	Yes, there is —
ASSISTANT	— and yours.

K	— thank you — You can explain how the officials who, quote unquote, arrested me while making off with my clothes —
ASSISTANT	Yes, your clothes —
INFO. OFFICER	We can get the ball rolling on that; which items have gone missing?
K	They haven't 'gone missing', they've been stolen; it doesn't matter —
ASSISTANT	If you could just make a list here —
K	Leave the clothes, I don't care; I want to / sort out …
ASSISTANT	We've started it now.
K	Are you here to help?
INFO. OFFICER	Of course.
K	Then tell me why I'm under arrest.
INFO. OFFICER	Every time.
ASSISTANT	I'll make a sign.
INFO. OFFICER	Mr K, to ensure a fair trial, the reason for the arrest is kept sealed until after the verdict. Can you imagine what the Higher Court would think of you if they knew why you'd been arrested?
ASSISTANT	Prejudicial.
K	So how am I supposed to I defend myself?
INFO. OFFICER	Mr K, we're not idiots; how can you be expected to mount a defence when you don't know why you're under arrest?
ASSISTANT	If you could keep writing your questions down …
DEFENDANT	For god's sake.
K	Shut up.

K *is overcome.*

INFO. OFFICER	Mr K? Has the nausea started already?
ASSISTANT	I think it's the breathing, too.
INFO. OFFICER	Shame; we've barely scratched the surface.
ASSISTANT	I think if he sits down for a while —

K   Get me out of here.

INFO. OFFICER   There's still a lot to cover —

K   Get me out.

ASSISTANT   We could pick it up next time, couldn't we?

INFO. OFFICER   I suppose we could.

K   What the hell is going on?

The INFORMATION OFFICER *and* ASSISTANT *lead* K *through the buildings.*

INFO. OFFICER   I'm glad you asked: the sun, being so much closer
                     to the roof beams than to the lower levels of the building,
                     has an unfortunate warming effect on those offices and
                     Courts situated in the upper layers and, since these are
                     building of some historical value and repute, it has
                     proven impossible to install any more modern
                     method of cooling than the installation of a

K   *gods, ee feel sick*   door at each of the Offices which, at times of
                                        particular heat, can be operated with a
           like oom seasick   flapping motion. A rota has been
                                        organised to ensure the efficient cooling
           like ee roll in heavy sea, of the building during the summer.
           oom roar from deep ee   Throughout the year, the combination
           pounden ears   of heat, absorbed and radiated by the
                                        wood of the beams, has a
           look ee smilen faces — how they   tremendously stifling effect upon
           all oom calm an compose, oom   the air, and it has been suggested
           beauty serene   that the Offices be relocated to a
                                                more temperate location. On
           how so they calm, ee   days when the traffic of
           room belching roll like on Defendants is heavy, it can be
           seasprings?   difficult to breathe, and we
                                         advise all such Defendants to
           Louder, please.   bring a small tank of oxygen,
           I can't … I can't hear   should they be planning a visit to
                                        the Offices in anything but the
           where ee taking him?   coldest of the winter months. In
           ee leading deeper into   addition, the petitioners will often hang
           bastard office bowels   washing up to dry, which can make an

55

how ee oom so weak?

oom let go im arms,
ee fall like rusty
plank. mayen ee
be wash overboard
an left on floor,
absorb in very
building fabric.
an Court take im
body oom bones, ee swallow
im whole, liken giant serpent coil under sea.

already humid environment even more so, and has been known to exacerbate pre-existing feelings of nausea. It is known that subsequent visits to the Offices have a much less debilitating effect upon the Defendant: very few experience any ill effects after their third visit. I hope you are feeling better now. Even though you are taking up space unnecessarily, we will certainly not hinder you in following the course of your case. And here we are ...

INFO. OFFICER   Come along, Mr K.

K   No, wait; the lawyer ...

INFO. OFFICER   You want to see your lawyer? Very well.

K, the INFORMATION OFFICER and the ASSISTANT arrive at GRACE's offices.

K   How did we get here?

INFO. OFFICER   Everything belongs to the Court.

CHERRY   Hello.

INFO. OFFICER   Cheryl.

CHERRY   Hello. Hi Josef.

K   Give these to Mrs Grace, please.

CHERRY   You're not coming in?

K   You have any news?

CHERRY   Depends if you're coming in. There's an underwater train in three hours; I know the guard –

K   I have to get back to work.

CHERRY   You said you'd come back.

Phone rings.

INFO. OFFICER   Come along, Mr K; let's just settle you in here, shall we?

K is left at the bank.

K   ee exhaust

       when ee last Rosa seen?

       home, im wait oom front door, open ee small crack

       into corridor, watchen Rosa door

       im never see

       ee dream of mouth oom neck

       thinken long fade an scent oom lips

Phone stop.

A series of brief, repeated scenes, with the assistance of RABENSTEIN, KAMINER & KULLYCH —

     K writes notes.

     K collects bundles of receipts, photographs & notes.

     K delivers bundles of paperwork to GRACE and CHERRY.

     K finds his paperwork scattered and discarded.

     K gathers up and reassembles his discarded notes.

Phone rings; KYLE enters.

KYLE   Josef?

      You all right?

K   I'm fine.

KYLE   Are you going to get that?

K   No, it's not important.

RABENSTEIN, KAMINER & KULLYCH point things out.

K   That's good. What do you need, Kyle?

KYLE   The Welsers are coming back in; you're going to have to grease
      the wheels with them.

Phone stops.

K   twenty-eight, im beggar grabbed oom street

       ee push oom desperate away

       im fall an head be crack oom pavement

       ee walk away

       but ee assault, and im only defend

KYLE	Well?
K	I'm sure you can handle it; you've been through enough of the files.
KYLE	What's that supposed to mean?
K	It just means I know when someone's been digging through my office.
KYLE	I picked up a couple of bits that were missing; I thought we should keep it all / together.
K	And you thought you'd come into my office when I wasn't here?
KYLE	You're never here, you're always off doing some personal errand. Someone's got to look after your clients.
K	I thought they were the bank's clients.
KYLE	You're making slack. It's got to be picked up.
K	And you should do it, should you?

ROSA enters.

ROSA	Hello, Josef. Hi Kyle.
KYLE	Hi.
K	*six months, im pick up clothes oom laundry an find ee Rosa knickers oom stuff small lacy black in pocket*
	then home, wrap tight around an fill whole fist of cloth with wet
ROSA	Is this a bad time?
K	No, of course not.
ROSA	Can I steal you for a minute?
K	Of course. Kyle, do you mind?

KYLE leaves. Phone rings.

K	How are you? How have you been?
ROSA	Fine. Busy. Work's … you know.
	Do you need to get that?

K	It's fine.
ROSA	And how are you?
K	I'm fine. Busy, too.
	You wanted to talk about something?
ROSA	Two things, really.

Phone stops.

K	See?
ROSA	Right.
	How's the arrest going?
K	The arrest? Oh, that; yes, that's all fine. Should be cleared up pretty soon.
ROSA	Oh, great. So your lawyer's good?
K	I'm thinking about letting her go, actually; doesn't seem to be doing much.
ROSA	It can seem like that. Dad said defence was like a swan; with the legs, under the surface. You know. Or an iceberg.
K	Your dad?
ROSA	He was a Magistrate for a while; there were some colleagues of his … if it's all going to be cleared up, maybe you won't need it, but I thought one of them might be able to help you. Not an official, exactly, but knowledgeable.
K	Not an official?
ROSA	He's an artist.
K	Right.
ROSA	He does a lot of work for the Court; not a lawyer or anything, but he hears things; he might know some other way to approach the whole thing.
K	You really think he can help?
ROSA	Just go and see him; don't get put off by the girl at the door.
K	Thank you.
ROSA	It's all right.

K	And did you get my letters?
ROSA	Yes, I did. That was the other thing.
K	Right.
ROSA	I'm sorry.
K	No, no, I didn't mean / to bother …
ROSA	Please, no; it's fine.
	I'm not really ready for anything … what you want. It's just not a good time, right now.
K	No, of course. Sorry to –
ROSA	It's fine; please.
K	All right, then.
ROSA	You will go and see him, won't you?
K	I think I will. If he can help, then I really don't need the lawyer.

KYLE *enters.*

KYLE	Rosa, I'm sorry, we need to get back to it.
K	Come on, Kyle, I don't think it's that / urgent.
KYLE	No, we really do.
K	Rosa, it's / not that …
ROSA	It's fine; take care.
K	Bye.

ROSA *leaves.*

K	You want to watch yourself.
KYLE	We're trying to build a book, here, you can can't have bits of skirt hanging around while you stare out the window. We're hunting elephants; the gun's loaded, get onboard.
K	Get onboard? Get onboard what, the elephant hunting boat?
KYLE	You'd rather be left to look through your porn?
K	They are legal documents –
KYLE	Oh, come on. Do what you want on your own time, but keep it at home; we meet clients here.

K   Don't you lecture me –

KYLE   No, listen. You keep on like this, it's not going to end well. If I
           hadn't read over that last lot, the whole thing would have gone
           south before you even knew about it.

K   It's not a senior member of staff's job to check over paperwork;
           I delegated, and left you to deal / with it.

KYLE   You didn't delegate, you were going to hand it over as was. You
           want to keep making me look good, that's fine with me; I'm just
           trying to help you.

K   You should talk less.

KYLE   Jesus. Smarten yourself up; have some pride.

KYLE *leaves.*

K   *age eleven im take ee mother bra from wash, an*
           wrap oom round ee little cock

           stupid, child, ee not know what im do

           nineteen

           ee spy oom housemate bedroom with mirror an
           keyhole

           watch her im fingers push an push

           tears ee face

           ee watch oom keyhole

           sure no guilt if no one hurt?

K *arrives at* GRACE'S *offices.*

GRACE   Josef, how good to see you; I trust your submissions are / going
           well.

K   I appreciate your efforts, Mrs Grace; but as of this moment, you
           no longer represent my legal interests.

GRACE   Interesting tactic. Let's think this through.

K   I've already thought it through.

GRACE   I'm not so sure you / have.

K   When we first met, I wasn't even slightly concerned about being
           under arrest, and I thought you'd make sure I didn't have to

be. But now, I spend all my time worrying about the case, and about how little you're doing about it.

CHERRY	Josef, don't talk like this —
GRACE	How little I do?
K	You haven't even asked me what happened at the arrest, let alone the hearing.
GRACE	I'm amazed at how successful you've been. The Law is a rarefied plane, Mr K, and I have earned my reputation.
K	Can I see my petition?
GRACE	It's been dealt with appropriately.
K	By throwing it into the street?
GRACE	All elements have been thrown where they will be most efficacious. I can assure you the work involved is excruciatingly intense.
K	Then allow me to reduce your burden. Give it back, I'll pursue it on my own.
GRACE	You may have misunderstood, Mr K. I have always stressed the importance of your writing your petition, but I have never promised you anyone would read it; the Higher Court doesn't concern itself with these sorts of things.
K	You said you couldn't get to the Higher Court.
GRACE	I said I couldn't get you to the Higher Court.
K	I think we're done.
GRACE	Cheryl, call Block in here.
CHERRY	Block. Block, come here; your lawyer wants you.
GRACE	You've been treated too kindly, and you undervalue the nature of my work; you should see what other defendants go through to secure my valuable assistance.
K	Just give me the papers.

BLOCK *enters.*

BLOCK	You called, Mrs Grace?
K	I know you.

BLOCK	I don't think so.
GRACE	Then you should be introduced. Block, tell Mr K why you're here.
BLOCK	Of course, ma'am. Gather, then, if you please, to hear The Most Lamentable Tale of Block the Accountant.
CHERRY	The Court likes it when they put a bit of drama into it.
BLOCK	My trial begins with the death of my fiancée, eighteen months ago, following a brief illness. Wracked with grief, I return from the hospital to find three men waiting to inform me of my arrest; I am too exhausted to ask for more details, and simply accept their words before retiring to bed. The next day, I am summoned to attend my first hearing, and realise, during the course of this interrogation, that I must accept the inevitability of my situation, and dedicate myself to ensuring that I remain in control. Since then, I have laboured each and every day under the shadow of this accusation, compiling the petition with which I intend to exonerate myself, engaging the services of the most distinguished lawyer, spending every moment in vigilant defence of my innocence.
	My fiancée would not wish me to crumble under the weight of this indignity; to honour her memory, I must employ the full force of my abilities; and today, here, I press on with my requests to have my petition heard. Thank you.
CHERRY	Sorry; the sad ones always get me.
GRACE	You've been practising.
BLOCK	Of course, ma'am.
GRACE	Good. Now what sort of time is this?
BLOCK	You only just called me.
GRACE	It's an inconvenient time; where were you earlier?
BLOCK	Of course, ma'am, please accept my apologies.
GRACE	All right; that'll be all.
BLOCK	Since I'm here, is there any news on my case?
GRACE	Did I mention any?

BLOCK	No.
GRACE	As it happens, I did have a croissant with an old friend from the third circle the other day; I suppose you'd like to know what I learnt.
BLOCK	Yes, very much.
GRACE	Then perhaps you should ask one of your other lawyers what he said. Oh yes, I know about your other lawyers, Block, I know all about them.
BLOCK	No, please, they don't hold a candle to / what you …
GRACE	That's quite right: they don't, not a single, flimsy, birthday cake candle. Not one of your charlatans knows which backstreet bar is frequented by their old friend the judge, and how many glasses of sherry it will take to loosen his horrible little lips from their grip around his secrets. Do they?
BLOCK	Of course, Mrs Grace, I'm ashamed to think how this must look to you –
K	He's only doing it because you're doing nothing.
CHERRY	Don't –
BLOCK	How dare you? She is brilliant, and only puts up with my piffling little case out of the goodness of her heart; I should have you flogged.
K	I'm not the one destroying your life –
CHERRY	Josef, please –
GRACE	Quiet, all of you. Cheryl: how has he been today?

CHERRY *gestures to a kennel.*

CHERRY	In there, going through his papers, same as usual.
BLOCK	I want to make everything as clear as possible for you, ma'am.
K	You live in there?
BLOCK	This, sir, is how a trial is conducted; if you don't care enough to dedicate yourself to it, I'm sure you'll face the consequences soon enough.
GRACE	What are you, Block?

BLOCK	I am your humble and devoted servant, ma'am.
GRACE	Put your tongue out. Further; good. Are you my dog?
BLOCK	Of course, ma'am.
GRACE	Good. Lick. That's good. Good boy. You are a good client, aren't you? Who's a good client? Who's a good client?
BLOCK	I am.
K	Jesus.
GRACE	Roll over. Now, Josef. You see?
	Speak.

BLOCK *barks.*

GRACE	The Court requires a certain humility; without it, your case is certainly doomed. This is what a client looks like: he understands that whatever's asked is more than reasonable for what I provide. You see how well you've been treated?
K	You make me sick.
CHERRY	Josef, just do what she wants; I can help you with / it all …
K	Get off me. We're done, here. I'll submit it myself, and I'm going to see someone who can actually help me.

BLOCK *snarls and lunges at* K.

GRACE	He can't help, you know.
CHERRY	Come back, please, you can still get out of this; just show her you can be humble if you / need to …
K	This isn't humility, it's slavery –

BLOCK *lunges at* K.

GRACE	Down. If you're so sure you know better, then get out. Down. Good boy. Sing.

BLOCK *howls.*

CHERRY	Josef.

K *leaves.*

K	*dam dogs; always dogs*
	twenty-three; she be unsure engagement

> *an Josef, ee shoulder for crying, an soon she use ee*
> *mouth an hands all over, for all night*
>
> *an then*
>
> *ignore ee letters, telephone, knockings*
>
> *soon, ee stop complete*
>
> *oom never see again*
>
> *im hear they snarl, howl oom window*
>
> *ee closer now?*

K arrives at TUDOR's workshop.

DEFENDANT	There's a queue.
K	I'm here to see Tudor.
DEFENDANT	We all are.
GIRL	Mister.
K	So I'm in the right place?
DEFENDANT	No. That's the back.
K	I'm not here for that.
DEFENDANT	Plenty of girls.
GIRL	Hi.
K	Hello. He's expecting me; do you mind if I go in?
DEFENDANT	I've been here for hours; I've got to get back to work.
GIRL	Hey, Josef. Come on.
K	Get off.

TUDOR enters.

TUDOR	Next.
DEFENDANT	Finally.
K	Excuse me, Rosa said I –
TUDOR	Josef K? You were supposed to be here an hour and five minutes ago.
K	I'm here now.
TUDOR	Come on.

K	Thank you for seeing me –
TUDOR	You, leave him alone.
K	What are they here for?
TUDOR	This. Or that. Sometimes both.
GIRL	Are you going to do him?
K	No, he's not.
GIRL	Got to get it sometime. Can I watch?
K	Miss, I know what you're offering, but it's not why I'm here.
GIRL	Yeah, but can I watch?
TUDOR	Both of you, shut up.

TUDOR *tattoos the* DEFENDANT.

K	Are you under arrest, then?
TUDOR	Don't talk to him. Yes, he is.
K	What's he having?
TUDOR	That's not how it works. The Law's already found the guilt; all I do is reveal it. Anyone can learn the officials' badges and whatnot, but reading the guilty, that's black arts. Easy if you know what you're looking for. If you're around it long enough.
	Sit still.
K	And you do everyone?
TUDOR	Defendants, officials, judges, lawyers, I see them all.
K	I have to say, I was starting to think this was all hopeless; it's a relief to find someone who's not part of the Court –
GIRL	Everything belongs to the Court.
K	But you can help?
GIRL	So, Josef. What did you do?
TUDOR	Don't pester the customers.
K	I'm not a customer.
GIRL	'course you're not.
TUDOR	Leave him alone.

	You're done. Pay the girl.
K	He has to pay?
TUDOR	Someone always has to pay.
DEFENDANT	What's the verdict?
TUDOR	See for yourself.

DEFENDANT *looks at his tattoo, and leaves.*

K	What was it?
TUDOR	You don't ask.
GIRL	Come on, strip.
K	I told you, I'm not here for that. Or that.
TUDOR	You'll only have to come back. We can talk while I do you.
K	Do I have a choice?
TUDOR	The Court always offers you a choice.

K strips.

GIRL	I knew it.
K	How big will it be?
TUDOR	Depends.

TUDOR *tattoos* K.

TUDOR	All right, you listening? They don't tell anyone about it, but once you've been arrested, there's only three ways you're getting out; Actual Innocence, Apparent Innocence and Protraction.
K	And guilty?
TUDOR	Four, then.
	There's only stories about Actual Innocence; when that happens, they destroy all the files, the notes from the arrest and the hearings, anything about it even happening, all gone. You're free.
	Little pinch.
K	All right, good; so how do we persuade them I'm innocent?
TUDOR	You can't. It's only in stories.
K	Then how do you know it's even possible?

TUDOR	Keep still.
	Option two's much more likely; Apparent Innocence.
K	More likely than 'completely impossible'?
TUDOR	That sort of thing won't help. They add a note to your file saying you're Apparently Innocent, and you carry on with your life. It looks like Actual Innocence, you might even feel Innocent; but you're not. They never forget. Your case stays in circulation, and a judge can have you arrested whenever he likes. It could take years, or it might never happen, or you might go home thinking you're innocent, and find the guards waiting.
K	It's just sounds now.
TUDOR	What?
K	Innocence; you've said it too much, it's just a funny sound.
	Innocence innocence innocence innocence innocence innocence.
GIRL	Innocence.
TUDOR	Actual Innocence –
	I wish you hadn't said that.
K	I feel sick.
TUDOR	Put your head down.
	Option three, what we call 'Protraction'. Everyone wants to be found innocent, but everyone can manage Protraction, with a bit of effort. You've got to game them: you get to know the right judges, keep them close, make sure they owe you favours, and you cash them in to make sure your case goes nowhere. They can keep it tied up, so it never reaches a verdict, and you can't be found guilty.
K	Or innocent.
TUDOR	That too.
K	You could replace the whole thing with a couple of hangmen.
TUDOR	Hardly fair on people who haven't done anything. That's what we should go for. Keep still, I told you.

K	I can't convince them I'm innocent?
TUDOR	Not enough to get you acquitted, and not in the Court; but there's other ways. Technically, if you're innocent, you have to be found innocent, and technically judges are incorruptible. In reality, innocent men are found guilty all the time.
K	And judges …?
TUDOR	Are not incorruptible. Protraction; you want my advice, that's what we'll do. You've been doing the petition?
K	Yes.
TUDOR	You want to keep it with you; you're screwed without it. The number of cases that are lost because of missing petitions.
	All right. Done; part of the system, now.

K *looks at his tattoo.*

K	What? What is it? I can't see it.
TUDOR	Keep trying. Next.
GIRL	Can I put the bandage on?
TUDOR	Go on.

GIRL *bandages* K.

K	So what happens now?
TUDOR	Rosa wants me to help you, so I'll help if you want. Protraction's my advice. Have a think about it, but don't take too long.
	That way.

K *sees the Court offices.*

K	What … what is this?
TUDOR	The offices? You knew about them.
K	I thought this place was different.
TUDOR	Everything belongs to the Court. You know your way?
K	Yes.
TUDOR	Next.
GIRL	Bye, Josef.

TUDOR Don't take too long.

K leaves.

K *calm*

ee musten calm

im all belong to Court, ee now obvious

also ee mark permanent, now, ee also belong oom Court

ee only hopen petition

yes, clear

ee present im petition alone, list all ee fault an error, purge all from im mind, fallen knees an throw ee mercy

KYLE enters.

KYLE Jesus, what happened to you? Are you bleeding?

K Not now.

KYLE Yes, now; they'll be here in a minute. You can't have forgotten again.

K They'll wait.

KYLE They're keeping the whole damned company afloat, they're not going to wait.

K Make them.

KYLE What is all this?

K It's personal.

KYLE You've got to be kidding me.

K Do I look like I'm kidding?

KYLE Yes. Look at yourself.

K Just get out; I'm busy.

KYLE I'm not going; they're expecting to see a senior member of management, and they're not going to sign without one. I'm stopped out on you screwing this up –

K Get out.

KYLE	We … don't make me do this.
K	You're going to drag me out there? Go and do your job.
KYLE	I'm doing my job; do yours. Christ, what is this that's so important? You find it lining a wheelie bin?
K	Put it down. It's a petition. I'm serious.
KYLE	Like a legal thing? Seriously, you're working on personal legal papers at work?
K	Not working on –
KYLE	This is … I can't let this slide; I'm sorry, I really am.
K	Put it down.
KYLE	I can't do it; we're talking about millions off the top here, and I'm not going to lose out because of you. What are you thinking? Jesus, the conflict of interest alone's enough to bury / us.
K	What conflict of interest? They're not company clients, where's / the conflict?
KYLE	Everything belongs to the Court.
K	What did you say?

Phone stops.

K	What did you say?
KYLE	This could fuck you right now.

K and KYLE fight; office workers separate them.

K	What did you say?
KYLE	Get him off me.
K	What did / you say?
KYLE	It's fine, it's fine, it's / nothing.
K	Get off me.

K snaps and snarls.

KYLE	I'm all right, just get him out of here. Everything's fine. You happy now, are you? Get him out.

K	I'm not going anywhere without my petition; it is my personal / property …
KYLE	They'll send it. It's fine; get back, there's nothing to see.
	Just go; they're not going to let you back in there.
K	I've got to have it.
	Please.
KYLE	You know you're not getting in. Go and see a doctor, get your eye sorted out.
K	Are you and Rosa … ?
KYLE	What?
K	You know. Are you?
	Are you?
KYLE	Yes. Happy? She thought it might tip you over the edge, but since it's clearly too late for that, yes. You know when it happened? Glad you asked: she came to that thing on the boat last year, because you, yes, because you were going to be there. And you didn't come, did you? So we got talking because she didn't know a single person there, and one thing led to another, like it does, and now here we are, and you know what? I'm really glad you're this much of a self-involved cunt, because it means I'm going to marry the girl you were too scared to talk to, and that you're going to die alone.
K	*twenty*
	im tell ee mother im glad ee father dead
	sit an watch as oom three hours cry
	You're going to marry her?
KYLE	Go and see a doctor.

K leaves.

TIFFANY dances for K.

K	*seventeen ee long friend David break in front*
	say ee love an cannot live without
	an im laugh ee away
	an ee go

DOCTOR *enters.*

DOCTOR	Cold out, eh?
	It's cold out.
K	Yes.
DOCTOR	Coldest since records began.
K	*an later, police van ee to hospital, lights a-flash*
	lift to drawer room, an pull back sheet oom face
	ask ee 'is this, is it, is this?'
	ee face be broke oom jump from window
	im eye be missed
	ee must oom stare for half minute, before im yes
	ee feel like weeks
DOCTOR	You're Josef K.
K	Yes.
DOCTOR	I thought I'd find you here. Is that your girl up there?
K	Tiffany? Sort of. Mine, and others'. Is there any point asking how you know who I am?
DOCTOR	Everything belongs to the Court. I'm here for your physical. That eye looks a little painful; we should change the dressing on that, too. Come on, strip. How are you feeling in yourself?
K	I've been better.

DOCTOR *puts a stethoscope to* K's *chest.*

DOCTOR	And your trial? How do you think that's going to end?
K	I used to think it'd be fine, but … I don't know. Do you?
DOCTOR	Me? No. Breathe in. It's not looking too promising, though, is it
K	I wouldn't know.
DOCTOR	And out. Chest sounds good. It's not looking promising because they think you're guilty. Heart's fine.

DOCTOR *puts a blood pressure cuff on* K.

K	You can't be just guilty; you've got to be guilty of something.

DOCTOR	That's what guilty people always say. One-ten over seventy ...
K	Is that all right?
DOCTOR	It's fine. Say ahh.
K	Ahh.
DOCTOR	Ok. Let's change that dressing. Ha.
K	What?
DOCTOR	It's nothing. Temperature's fine. Little ovular mole there; doesn't look like anything to worry about.
	Everything seems normal. Is there anything you're concerned about? Any pain?
K	Some pain.
DOCTOR	How would you describe it?
K	It doesn't matter.
DOCTOR	If you're sure. Is there anything you want to talk about?
K	No.
DOCTOR	All right. Your eye's a little swollen, so ice for that; you can take that dressing off in a couple of hours, as well. Clean bill of health, apart from that.
K	Is that it?
DOCTOR	That's it.
K	Do you have to go?
DOCTOR	I can stay for a while, if you like.
K	Thank you.

K and DOCTOR watch TIFFANY.

DOCTOR	She's good, isn't she?
	Was there something you wanted to talk about?
K	Not really.
	I keep thinking what I could have done differently.
DOCTOR	Everything.
K	Would it have helped?

DOCTOR	I don't know. It was all only meant for you, after all.
K	What do they want from me?
DOCTOR	The Court? It doesn't want anything from you. It receives you when you come, and dismisses you when you go.

K *wakes up in bed.*

K   *an morning again; an almost woke ee up*

clothed for occasion, the great white hole, lord of all
surveys, ee audience await, an morning welcome in
one more year oom world of treacle wade.

hello neighbours, staren window still

not a wave

ee hearen howl an pant, close by

an not afraid

listen birds, look back blank oom neighbour
windows, an wait ee oom new day

Come on, come in.

MALE GUARD and FEMALE GUARD enter; they have the heads of dogs.

K   Well, happy birthday to me.

Good evening.

You're here for me? Don't worry, no one's in.

There's no hurry, I take it? I can get dressed?

It's strange: at the beginning I couldn't wait to end it all; now I just want it to start again.

Is there someone else out there?

What happened? There was a point, wasn't there – if it's ... there was a point, there was somewhere when it could have been different, wasn't there?

It's just, I've been over it, and I can't see it.

There was something I could have said, is that it? Of course there was, but would it – I could have objected, there was some argument I could have made? Or someone, maybe? The judge I never met, is that it?

There is someone out there. Not Rosa? No? I thought I saw her. Who's out there?

Of course, yes; everyone is.

an what ee say now, after?

that Josef K, im nothing learn for whole year arrest?

sayen im throw away all ee chance oom understand?

all opportunity thrown for escape?

may be

ee musten calm; more calm, ee better conclusion

no point oom struggle

welcome, watchen all

hopen Rosa not ee find

K is hanged.

end.

also by Nick Gill

mirror teeth
9781849431927

fiji land
9781783190904

WWW.OBERONBOOKS.COM

Follow us on www.twitter.com/@oberonbooks
& www.facebook.com/OberonBooksLondon